On Palace Green

On Palace Green

A Wedding in Williamsburg, 1807, in the
letters of those who were there.

P. J. Heffernan

PATRICK J HEFFERNAN

ISBN-13: 9781547246496
ISBN-10: 1547246499
Library of Congress Control Number: 2017909209
CreateSpace Independent Publishing Platform
North Charleston, South Carolina

To Karin

May Eternal Light shine upon her

Whose ever tender light warmed all in her life

Introduction

In my work I have the privilege of reading hundreds of historic letters preserved in libraries and other archives. There is an excitement in being handed a folder of unseen letters from the past. It is akin to receiving a box containing unknown gifts. Before opening the folder, I know that each letter in it will be new to me; and, more often than not, will bring some delight all its own. The penned words may unravel an historical puzzle I have been working on, or reveal a surprising detail, or provoke a rethink of a familiar character. Furthermore, the writing is often entertaining or eloquent in its own right. Research has many rewards but, for me, the delight of reading letters from the past is the most special.

I have composed this small book to enable others to experience that same delight. Transcribed in full is an exchange of fifty-six letters written in the winter of 1806–1807 by persons whom most readers are not likely to know. There are no very famous persons in the story, though many were importantly involved in shaping the new nation—and the central event is simply a proposal of marriage. Not one of the letters is from either of the love-struck pair to the other; for though some were written, none have been found. So these are not love letters. They are, however, loving, and interesting, and entertaining letters in all sorts of ways. It is the humanity and beauty of the correspondence, not the importance or drama of the events, that encouraged me to make it available to others.

I believe that handwritten personal letters have a distinct quality that appeals to most readers. Anyone who has labored over a personal letter knows that there is a unique challenge and perhaps pleasure that comes from writing down what we think. We are especially aware of the reader. We want to say things sincerely, or charmingly, or wittily. We cannot easily revise our thoughts once they are inked to a page. We are pleased or dismayed by our handwriting, choice of words, and so forth. All of these elements enter into the delight that comes from reading personal letters. They are both compositions and mirrors in which their writers are reflected.

Additional elements prompted me to assemble this collection. First among them is that the story is true. The people are real and the events actually happened. Secondly, it is told in the words of those who lived it. It is thus a chronicle of the *thoughts and feelings of those caught up in the events*, as distinct from a simple record of the events themselves. It is composed from the material of diaries, not newspapers. The people in the story are not my creations, and their story is told not by me but by them, *in their own words*.

The correspondence reveals the love, hopes, worries, and joys of a father for his daughter, of a mother for her son, of brothers for each other, of friends for all involved, and at the center of it all of a young man for a young woman. Because all of these persons put their thoughts and feelings into writing, their sentiments did not vanish the moment after they were expressed, as in speech. Rather, what they thought and said remains for us to enjoy today, just as it was in their day by the correspondents, all of whom were alive when Washington became the first president of the United States. It is as if we are looking over the shoulders of these members of the new republic, while they anxiously penned or opened a letter.

Finally, the events largely took place in a setting that, most remarkably, has also been preserved: Colonial Williamsburg. Many of the streets traveled by horses and coaches then are traveled by the same today. The greens and sidewalks walked upon by the people in the story can still be walked upon by us. Many of the homes and other buildings that they visited and mentioned in their letters stand today, just as they did in the winter of 1806-1807. The most important home in the story, that of St. George Tucker on the Palace Green, is among them. It was the favored gathering place for all family and friends then, and the basis for the title of this book now.

Thus we have the rare treat that both the sentiments and the scenes of a family story, which unfolded in the early years of our new nation, have been preserved. We are not only able to enter into the thoughts of the family members and their friends, but also into some of the very rooms where they once enjoyed each other's company.

Reading this collection of letters is much like reading the script of a stage play. All of the people in it arrive from behind a curtain and then speak their parts. Some have many lines; others appear just once and are gone. With that similarity in mind, I have written short descriptions of the main characters, like those found in theater programs. Some of these are placed in the text where the person first appears. All can be found at the back of the book. These may help readers keep track of who is who, and how they relate to each other.

Though it would never have crossed their minds that they would one day do this, it is time to let the residents and friends of the house on Palace Green tell their story to us.

A Bit of Background

In November 1788, at age twenty-seven, George Carter died. He died without a will, leaving behind his wife of just four years, Lelia Skipwith Carter, and his two children, Charles and Mary. Lelia was twenty-two, Charles three, and Mary not yet one.

George Carter also left behind the Corotoman estate, which by law was inherited by Charles and Mary. At the time of their father's death it encompassed about 6200 acres on the neck of land formed by the waters of the Rappahannock River on the south, the Corotoman River on the west, and Carter's Creek on the east. Though less than thirty-five miles from Williamsburg as the crow flies, the estate was greatly isolated from it by two rivers (the Rappahannock and, further south, the York) and very much removed socially. Whereas Corotoman's nearby town of Kilmarnock then contained little more than an ordinary and its new (1805) post office, Williamsburg was an old and bustling town that contained the College of William & Mary, the former Governor's Palace from colonial days, the former Capitol that had served the colony until 1780, numerous shops and taverns, a weekly newspaper and more. In the terms of the day, Williamsburg was the 'old city' and Kilmarnock was little more than a crossroads, which indeed (with a capital 'C') had been its name until the 1760s.

Also listed in George Carter's inventory was a community of 142 slaves, almost a third of them children. The slaves might well have been worth more than the land. Indeed, slaves were generally so critical to the value of Virginia's farmlands that in 1727 the Virginia Assembly passed a statute intended to prevent administrators of estates from selling inherited slaves separately from inherited land. Charles and Mary thus became very wealthy in their infancy as owners of one of Virginia's oldest and largest plantations, meaning the land and slaves, with a guardian appointed to protect their inheritance until their adulthood.

Their lives took another major turn three years later when their mother accepted the proposal of marriage from St. George Tucker, a distinguished jurist from Williamsburg. Tucker was widowed in the same year as Lelia when his first wife, Frances Bland (Randolph) Tucker, died. Hence St. George Tucker and Lelia Skipwith Carter both began their second marriages when they were wed at Corotoman in October of 1791.

Lelia, Mary and Charles moved at once to Tucker's house on the Palace Green in Williamsburg, where fifteen years later the story told in these letters took place. In their new home Charles and Mary joined Tucker's five children by Frances who were already there, and also became the youngest relations of three grown children of the now extensive Tucker family.

For Frances too had married St. George as a widow with children from *her* first marriage—Richard, Theodorick, and John Randolph. Those three young men had left home by 1791 to pursue their careers. It is not important to remember all the members of the Palace Green household, but simply to know that four prominent Virginia families were now united in it— the original Tuckers and Randolphs were now joined by the Carters and Skipwiths.

The story opens with St. George Tucker (55) and William Cabell (35) in Richmond, from where his brother Joseph Carrington Cabell (27) had just departed for Williamsburg. William and his wife Agnes were among the few who knew the purpose of Joseph's journey: to make a proposal of marriage. Lelia (40) was there in the Tucker home along with her daughter Mary, usually called "Polly," who was now eighteen—and the object of Joseph's affections. Polly's older brother Charles (20) was in Paris, having moved there from Edinburgh where his medical studies had begun in 1805. An ocean journey by ship away, he was inevitably unaware of anything going on at home until months after it occurred.

Portrait of Joseph Carrington Cabell. Courtesy of Special Collections, University of Virginia Library[1]

Letter 1: From Joseph Cabell in Williamsburg to William & Agnes Cabell in Richmond[a]

Williamsburg, 23rd Oct 1806

Dear Governor and Governess,

Tho' my present situation is not the most favorable for writing, yet I deem it my duty to inform you how I come on in the world of gallantry.

The night I left you was to me a very uncomfortable one. At the Eagle I was, according to the custom of our country, ushered into a common bed-room for the stage passengers. Solitude would have been much more congenial to the existing disposition of my mind. Among the passengers were Mr. Mead [Meade], brother to Mrs. Peyton Randolph, and Mr. Page, whose elder brother married Miss Nicholson: both of them students of Wm. & Mary. Soon after we had got to bed, in came a drunken party of young men, which they [Meade & Page] had just left, to rouse & call them again to the bowl. In this group the principal figure was a huge young man of the name of Smith, from Manchester, and the son of Mr. Obey Smith, of that place, who you know, was a distant relation of ours. After rolling over first one acquaintance & then another, and ruling in affected drunkenness thro' the room, he retired with his band, and left us to our repose. I am told he is an amiable sensible young man. He has yet to learn however the indecency of bursting into a room, & making it the scene of midnight revels, when not exclusively occupied by intimate friends; & reflection will at a future day teach him to shudder at the effect, which such an event would produce on the reputation of Virginia, had my bed contained some splenetic, generalizing traveler.

The coffee I had taken with you, & the tea I had drunk at Mr. Tucker's would of themselves have banished sleep, but they were powerfully aided by the tremendous snoring of a Capt. Jones from Hampton, who occupied the bed contiguous to mine. The motive of my journey was, however, the great cause of my watching thro' the silence of the night. The image of the girl I love, was constantly flitting around my bed. "Three times did I attempt to embrace it; three times did it vanish in air." At length, about two in the morning, I sunk to sleep. At three, we all sprang up at the sound of the Driver's horn. You know what a cold, driving rain from the east, had commenced in the course of the night. I was too old a traveller not to secure myself one of the back seats, by dressing hastily, and hurrying into the stage: and I felt myself somewhat entitled to it, as I was first on the way-bill; tho' in this country the preference of places is not regulated, as in France, by the time at which they are engaged. The remnant of the night seemed to me excessively long. Tho' occupying the best part of the carriage, I could not avoid the reflection, that we have yet to make many improvements in Virginia, to bring us to a level, with France & England, in respect to the conveniencies of civilized life. Could any thing, for example, appear more shocking to an inhabitant of one of those countries, than for a delicate female to be called from a warm bed, several hours before day; to set out on a journey in a dreadful spell of weather, in an American stage, open as it is before, & with a current of air driving constantly on the passengers. I remember how strongly this idea presented itself to my mind, even before I went to Europe, when we travelled this rout on our way to Charleston; and again when I passed it on my way to France. In both of those instances, I felt the effects for several days after I got to Norfolk. In every country, there is an affinity between the peculiar circumstances of the society, the existence of particular customs; and we ought to distinguish between defects arising out of the state of the country, those which owe their continuance to the negligence of the people. Our population is yet too thin, and dispersed, to admit of good roads; till the roads shall be improved, the present coarse, uncomfortable stages will continue in use; but I see no reason why they should not secure travellers against robbery, by attaching their baggage to the carriage, with a chain instead of a rope; and why they should not cover their trunks with, and keep out the rain from the wardrobes of young men bound on amorous expeditions. We arrived and breakfasted about sunrise, at the house on this side of Bottom's Bridge, which has long been as notorious for good fried chickens, as Virginia is for fried bacon and eggs. By this time, we had all become as well acquainted, and assumed a relative deportment towards each other, as perfectly as if we had been a month together in a tour. Mead is a young man of an amiable character, without literary pretentions, and of easy, unpolished manners. Page possesses nearly the same character, with more diffidence and restraint. We had with us a son of Ben Pollard of Norfolk, teller of the Bank there, with whom I boarded at Rainbows, when on my way to France. He is by no means interesting in point of character, talents, or manners, as the former; a few words in relation to Bishop Madison, under whose direction he had studied two years, displayed to me the class of young man to which he belonged. "The Bishop", said he, "is a selfish old scoundrel, and is the cause of the downfall of the College." Such a remark would at all times suffice to make me pass by its author in a crowd. It lifts the curtain from his character and displays him at full length. But from further conversation with Pollard, I found that his defects arose, from the want of wise superintendence to correct his deviations, and direct him in the right way. Indeed every step I take in Virginia, displays to my view the elements of a great character, which only await cultivation & a proper direction, to astonish the world. Jones of Hampton, is an old sea-captain, but now a merchant, and tho' an illiterate man, possesses a strong mind, and fine vein of humor. He left his Father at the age of eleven years, and has since been cast on a most every shore. He related to me an incident respecting the loss of Mrs. Cowper, the wife of Turk Cowper, which touched my feelings to the quick. The steward of Captain Drummonds packet, is a black man, belonging to Hampton, and is one of the few who escaped. He says that after being three days on the wreck, and almost famished, he dived into the cabin, in order to get some biscuit out of one of the Lockers; and he saw Mrs. Cowper sitting in an easy posture, with one of her arms around a post, and two beautiful French maids lying dead at her feet. Can any thing more strongly display the resignation, the innocence, the helplessness of the female character! Could the imagination find a more touching incident to close the last scene of an amiable & admired woman!

At New Kent Court-house we took up the Brother of Julius Dandridge, who has gone on a short trip to Norfolk. We were there also joined by the wife of the Tavern Keeper at the place called Gaddys, sixteen miles above Williamsburg: she had a little son a few years old with her, who delighted us on arriving there, by running about the room like a bird let out of a cage, and the ardor he discovered on meeting an older brother.

About three o'clock, the steeple of the old church in Williamsburg appeared at a distance. This was once the signal to me for violent emotions, and you would suppose would have proven so again by recalling recollections of the past. My mind was too much engaged about the present, to think of the past: and I am too old an adventurer not to be calm and collected even on my present interesting expedition. I was not however sorry that the inclemency of the weather caused us to enter the old city with closed curtains. It was diverting to observe a meeting between the students in the stage, and a black, hideous servant, who is a great favorite in the College, and lives with the students of the present day, on the most familiar and friendly terms. Julius had taken a stand in the middle of the street not far from the College gate, in order to salute any of his old friends who might pass by. By G-d, Julius, how are, said the students. G-d d-n it, lads, how are you, said Julius, with the voice of a stentor.

On descending from the stage at the Rawleigh, I found a crowd of observers, as usual; and among them some attendants on the Court of Chancery; but I saw neither Mr. Wirts, nor anyone, who could conjecture the cause of my trip to the old city. Presently the Brother of George Tucker, popped in, and then I knew I 'stood confessed'. I asked two or three useless questions, in order to make way for another – "whether Mr. Brent had left Williamsburg." "He was to have gone this morning," said he, "but was prevented by the weather; but he will certainly go to-mor-row." If Lavater, or Upshaw, or either of you, had been present, you would have observed a change in my counte-nance. At that moment a cloud of anxiety took its flight. However there were still some doubts. As the weather was dreadful, I was cruelly obliged to spend the evening in the Tavern: but I forwarded my packet of letters, with one from Mrs. Peyton Randolph, handed me by her brother. Young Mr. Tucker took charge of them with a message that I would call in the morning, and that I should be happy to see Mr. Brent before he left town. Brent came in about twilight, and I could gather the poor fellow's fate from the first glance. I immediately took him up stairs into my bed room, where I had a fire prepared, and informed him of the change in my mind since we had parted, and of the purport of my visit to Williamsburg: expressing at the same time much regret, at the idea of having rival pretensions with a friend on such an occasion. He as promptly replied that he was an unsuccessful candidate; and that he hoped I might be a more fortunate man. My mind at this observance must have resembled the face of a certain ventriloquist in Paris, who I saw smile on one side, and weep on the other. Brent's conduct was so liberal, so feeling, and so full of character, that I really sympathized with him; while at the same time I was delighted that he had not carried off the object of my pursuit. We slept together that night, after taking an oyster supper together, and parted the next morning in perfect friendship. He took the stage for Richmond, where he promised me to call on you.

The next day I walked thro the rain with young Mr. Mead to Mr. Tuckers. As I crossed the C. House Square, and entered the house I heaved two or three deep sighs. But George Tucker, soon appeared, followed by Miss P. [Polly] who looked more beautiful than I ever saw her. In a few minutes all agitation had disappeared, & we were all in high talk. Mrs. T. was confined to her room by a cold which she took in coming down: but as I left the house sent an invitation after us, to come to dinner at 3 o'clock, which you may be sure I did not refuse. I came on Mr. Moore's where I took up my quarters during my stay in town; and proceeded to the old Bishop's who was engaged in the College. I saw Mr. & Miss Madison, but have not called since owing to the state of the weather. On my return to Mr. Moore's, the old Lady in the course of conversation, informed me that Mrs. Skipwith had told her that I was expected down soon to see Miss P. and that Mrs. T. had confided this intelligence to her. I dined yesterday at the old Judge's in company with the Miss Birds [Byrds]. After dinner, George T. & myself happened alone, when in conversing about Brent, I informed him of my intentions; and told him I thought it unnecessary to say anything on the subject to Mr. or Mrs. Tucker, in which opinion he agreed with me. At this moment he delivered me an invitation to dine to day at <u>Col. Skipwith's</u>. I expressed to him my surprise & pleasure at this invitation, as I had always regretted the suspension of my intercourse with a family, to which I had been so much indebted for friendly attentions. He said every thing was forgotten: and I assured him I would attend with pleasure. We passed the evening at the Judge's, laughing and talking with the young ladies. I think my prospect favorable, and I am only waiting to get Miss P. as much into the notion of matrimony as myself to propose the question. I suppose it will be necessary to defer this for a week or two, out of respect to common forms, but the delay to me is oppressive, for I stand committed, and anxious for a termination of the affair. To-day I have kept close quarters, owing to a heavy rain: but in an hour or two I shall be dying in the presence of Miss P. who is now the empress of my soul. Courting in heavy rains, thro' deep mud, is hard work. However I dash thro' every difficulty to obtain the

*object I adore. Shew this to Upshaw in confidence, and
take care not to tell it to more than a dozen people.*
    Yours Sincerely,
    Joseph C. Cabell

Readers will need to decide for themselves whether Joseph's last
words to his brother were serious or sarcastic. Was he really asking William to share his news with just a few others, or conced-
ing with a smile that he had no hope of stopping his brother
from gleefully telling all the family and friends in Richmond
about his exploits in Williamsburg?

WILLIAM H. CABELL.

Portrait of William H. Cabell. Courtesy of Special
Collections, University of Virginia Library[2]

Many of the places mentioned in this letter have been preserved to this day: Bruton Parish Church, the Raleigh Tavern, and the Court House on its square can all be visited at Colonial Williamsburg. The homes of St. George Tucker and Col. Henry Skipwith, who was Lelia's uncle, stand there now as they did then on opposite sides of the Palace Green. Moore's, to which Cabell moved after his first night at the Raleigh, refers to the Market Square Tavern, then owned by James Moore. Though no longer a tavern, the building still stands near the Courthouse. Finally, the President's House for William & Mary College has been preserved and looks much as it did when it was Bishop James Madison's home. Having been the college's president since 1776, Madison (cousin of the U.S. President with the same name) was an old friend of St. George Tucker, and first met Cabell when he was a student.

William Brent, who was five years younger than Cabell, attended William & Mary in 1800, which is likely when the two first met. Not only did Brent and Cabell leave Richmond within days of each other to propose to Polly Carter, but it seems Cabell did so following a change of heart, after wishing Brent well on his solo mission! It is thus no wonder that Cabell was pleased that heavy rain caused the leather coverings to be rolled down over the windows of the stage as it sloshed into the Old City. Both intrigue and embarrassment were in play, with Cabell aware that, on the face of it, his mission was a monumental betrayal of his friend. He did not want to be seen just yet by Brent or anyone in his acquaintance.

But he was. The brother of George Tucker who immediately upset Cabell's hope to arrive undiscovered was quite certainly a cousin of St. George. George Tucker [the cousin] had emigrated from Bermuda to Williamsburg in 1795 at age twenty, studied law under St. George, and then moved to Richmond. It is of no consequence that we do not know his brother's name. But that he knew both Cabell and what was going on at the Tucker house *was* of consequence, for he was able to advise Cabell on the state of things there. Though not in Cabell's plan, it helped Cabell to bump into him right after he stepped off the stagecoach.

A stagecoach was little more than a wagon with shapely sides and a roof over it, seating six to twelve persons on two to four fixed benches set on the same level. One of those persons was the driver, who sat on the front bench, often with a passenger or two beside him. The three seats on the rearmost bench, one of which Cabell nabbed, had the advantages of a seatback and the best shelter from the wind and rain that could flow in from the open front. Only the arrival of a female passenger could cause a male occupant to give up a back seat.

The term 'stagecoach' derived from the fact that some journeys had to be done in stages, with the horses or driver or both being changed after traveling some distance. Whether such changes were routine for the near fifty-mile rough road journey between Richmond and Williamsburg is not clear. The journey itself was routine, with stagecoaches traveling between the two places daily, carrying both passengers and the mail. While diverse thoughts such as these occurred to Cabell, they could not distract him. Nor shall they further distract us.

Letter 2: From Joseph Cabell in Williamsburg to William Cabell in Richmond

Williamsburg, 26ᵗʰ Oct 1806

Dear Brother;

Polly Carter is my wife; she is your Sister; she is the daughter of my Mother. She engaged herself to me last evening. Today I am to apply for Mrs. Tucker's consent, who has been confined to her room since my arrival and provided she gives it, of which I believe there is no doubt, I shall send off a letter to the Judge by to-morrow's stage. Whether I shall await his reply, or whether I shall return with my friend Cocke to Surry, when he comes over on the 28ᵗʰ, I cannot now decide. I shall endeavor to bring the family into as short an engagement as possible, and return in a few days to Richmond. I am as completely happy in my engagement as man ever was. She is indeed a lovely girl. Her conduct last evening endeared her to me, if possible, more than ever. She has my most tender affection, and I am rich in hers. I am beyond doubt the man whom she prefers to all others ^= an idea which to me is worth the Indies. How happy am I that I am about to form a connexion with a woman, with whom all my friends will be pleased, who lives in the very bosom of them all, and who belongs to so respectable a family, in which I have been intimate for so many years. I have not now time enough to give vent to my feelings on this subject. In another letter, or on another occasion, I will mention some of the incidents which have occurred since the date of my last. I will write shortly to my Mother to make known to her what is going on. Shew this to my Sister; and also to our friend Upshaw, who not only has contributed to save my life abroad, but to render it happy at home. You are all miserable creatures compared to me at present. I am too happy to write any longer.

> *Yours sincerely,*
> *Joseph C. Cabell.*

P.S. Mrs. T. has given her approbation, on condition that I obtain Judge Tucker's and my Mother's and I consequently write to them both, by the same mail which brings you this.

After the interview of this morning, I have determined to remain here about a week longer, before I return to Richmond, and I will thank you to write me as soon as possible your opinion as to the time of my marriage. I think the family would certainly consent to its taking place at Christmas, but I have proposed the 1st Dec. and should like to know your ideas as to the convenience of those two periods.

> *Yours affectionately.*
> *J. C. Cabell.*

The Upshaw with whom Cabell wished his good news to be shared was Dr. William Upshaw, who had provided Cabell with a room in Paris and joined him on some of his travels when the two Virginians were abroad in France just a few years earlier. From what Cabell says in this letter, Upshaw may also have administered some medical care to him both in Paris and in Richmond.

For Joseph to tell his older brother that Polly was already his sister was hyperbole and exuberance. Even their engagement to each other was not assured until they had received the approval of the parents in both families. The custom of the day in the newly independent nation was that adult children were left free to choose their partners. But when a significant estate was involved on either side of the equation the consent of the woman's parents was expected socially; and if the woman was not yet twenty-one, the consent of her parent or guardian was required legally. Polly met both of those conditions.

On the other hand, in referring to Polly as William's sister, and not sister-in-law, Cabell was using one of the customary forms of their day. Relatives created through marriage were most often referred to in the same way as relatives created through birth. In most family communications, they were not distanced with the addition of "in-law." But in Cabell's next letter that distinction was recognized by him as important, and was used.

Letter 3: From Joseph Cabell in Williamsburg to St. George Tucker in Richmond

Williamsburg, 26ᵗʰ Oct 1806

My dear Sir;

Tho' the object of my visit to this city be intimately connected with your family, I did not deem it necessary to mention the subject to you before I left Richmond. It now, however, becomes requisite to break the silence between us. I came down with no other object in view, than to solicit the hand of your Daughter-in-law. I have met with the good fortune, on which my repose & happiness in life so materially depended. Mrs. Tucker has been so kind as to smile on our mutual affection. It remains only for you to consent to our union in order to consummate our happiness. I ardently beseech you, to permit me to draw closer the ties by which I have long been attached to your family, & to call you by the venerable title of Father, instead of the endearing term of Friend. Next to the idea of possessing Miss Carter as a companion for my future days, no circumstance could give me more happiness than that of finding such a companion, in the bosom of a circle of friends with whom I have grown old in habits of affection. I await your reply, with all the anxiety which its import and consequences ought naturally to inspire.

Your respectful friend.
Joseph C. Cabell.

Judge Tucker.
now in Richmond.

At this time, when mail was the fastest form of communication over a distance such as that between Richmond and Williamsburg, writers expected that their letters would be responded to within a day or two of being received. Thus Cabell knew that the earliest he was likely to learn St. George's response would be three days later, given the day's journey each way for letters carried by stagecoach. For urgent or important matters, writers commonly entrusted their letters to any known traveler who might be heading to (or near) the letter's destination on horseback or private coach. Slaves, too, often carried letters for their masters and waited for the response of the recipient in order to immediately carry it back. In this case St. George responded promptly, as expected.

Miniature Portrait of St. George Tucker. Courtesy of The Colonial Williamsburg Foundation, Museum Purchase, The Friends of Colonial Williamsburg Collections Fund.[3]

Letter 4: From St. George Tucker in Richmond to Joseph Cabell in Williamsburg

Richmond, 28th Oct 1806

Dear Sir;

I this morning received your favor of the 26th communicating the object of your Journey to Williamsburg. I flatter myself that during an acquaintance of several years you have received too many demonstrations of the most sincere esteem and friendship on my part, to suppose for a moment that you would ever meet with any repugnance on my side, to draw closer the ties which have attached us to each other and to exchange the endearing term of Friend for one still more endearing. — It is a flattering circumstance to me, that the relations in which we have stood to each other should in any measure contribute to quicken, or to gratify, your wishes & feelings in proposing to yourself a partner for life — and I receive, and reciprocate the Sentiment with great cordiality.

But, my dear Sir, there are two preliminaries which Candour requires I should immediately communicate, without which it will not be in my power to meet your wishes, or my own. The first is a positive assurance that our Child will be received with open Arms by your Family, & particularly your Mother. — Until this assurance is received we can never release her from our own Embraces.

The second arises out of my relative Situation to my adopted Child, who is most truly the Child of my tenderest Affections. — Long habituated to look upon her only as my own, my heart vibrates with every tender emotion on seeing her on the Eve of a Measure which is to determine her future happiness. Long experience & frequent & painful observation have determined me, whenever the Occasion should require, to interpose, as far as it is possible by any exertion of mine, between her, and one of those sad reverses of fortune that I have too often seen among Ladies in Virginia. — At present she is, and I thank Heaven, perfectly independent in respect to fortune. — It is my duty to preserve that independence to her, in Case she should happen to Survive you. I must therefore propose to you, (as I did to your friend Mr. Coalter, when I gave him my beloved Fanny,) that previous to her marriage her whole Fortune shall be settled upon her, and her heirs — thereby securing to her an Independence through life, without wishing to abridge you of the full enjoyment of the rents & profits; & Interest of whatever money there may be in the hands of the Administrator of her Uncle Edward Carter, who had the sole management of her property till his Death.

I beg you to be assured, my dear Sir, that this proposal proceeds from no personal Distrust: I made it to your friend Mr. Coalter, upon principle, for the reasons I have mentioned. And I make it to you, as I did to him, with Confidence that you cannot hesitate a moment to view it in its proper light, & to give that unequivocal pledge of an honourable, & disinterested Attachment to our beloved Child. These preliminaries complied with, you will receive from my hand the dearest pledge of my esteem and friendship that it is, or ever can be hereafter in my power to give to man. I beg to be favoured with as early an answer to this proposal as possible, and in the meantime remain, Dear Sir,

 Most warmly & affectionately your friend
 S: G: Tucker

Care of Mrs. Tucker
 L. Tucker, anxious that Mr. Cabell should have time to deliberate on the contents of the enclosed Letter, and also desirous that his reply should not by her detention of it, be postponed, hastens to send it to him — The Letter was sent open for the perusal and approbation of Mrs. T. — who, at the same time that she avows every corresponding sentiment of respect and perfect esteem for Mr. C. also avows her concurrence with Mr. T. in those measures which equally interest her daughter & Mr. C. —
 Lelia Tucker 29. Oct: 1806

St. George made his reply to Cabell via Lelia, who added her own postscripted message to it, siding with her husband in print, while also sympathizing with Joseph and supporting Polly in person. She then delivered the letter to the anxious suitor.

Some other background information, which would be understood by Cabell but possibly not by today's readers, deserves presentation. At the time of their father's death in 1788, both Polly and Charles were minors and would remain so until they reached age 21, or in Polly's case, until she married, if sooner.

Miniature Portrait of Lelia Skipwith Carter Tucker. Courtesy of
The Colonial Williamsburg Foundation, Museum Purchase,
The Friends of Colonial Williamsburg Collections Fund.[4]

Shortly after George Carter's death, Edward Carter, a younger
brother, was appointed administrator of his estate and guardian
of his two minor children. It was Edward's responsibility, not St.
George's, to manage Corotoman in such a way that its value was
preserved till the orphaned children came of age.

He had faithfully done so until the year before this exchange of letters. In November of 1806 Edward tragically died when a mill-bank on his own estate gave way beneath him. In law the administration of Corotoman and guardianship of Charles and Mary would now pass to the (as yet unknown) person appointed administrator of *Edward's* estate. Approval of Polly's marriage itself, however, like all else to do with her welfare day to day, belonged to St. George ever since his marriage to Lelia.

This letter invites the introduction of a key member of the cast:

John Coalter (b. 1769) At the time of this story John Coalter had been married to Polly's older stepsister, Ann Frances Bland Tucker (Fannie), since 1802. He was thus Polly's brother-in law. Coalter first met Fannie in 1788 when she was nine years old, and he had moved from his family's home in Augusta County to live with the Tuckers as a tutor. In exchange for this service, St. George arranged for him to study law at William & Mary, from which he obtained his law degree in 1790 and returned to Augusta to practice. Fannie was his third wife, the two preceding having died in child-birth. The Coalters gave St. George and Lelia their first grandchildren, Frances Lelia and Elizabeth.

At the time of Coalter's marriage to Fannie, St. George had stipulated that he create a legal document to protect the wealth that Fannie brought to their union. Under Virginia law the wife's assets passed entirely to the husband. Coalter understood and shared Tucker's view, based on his extensive courtroom experience, that this put married women in jeopardy of destitution, resulting from the misfortune or financial misconduct of their husbands. Accordingly, Coalter readily entered into a settlement (legal agreement) to protect Fannie, which Tucker now cited to Cabell as an example of what he now ought to do for Polly. Joseph again turned to his brother for advice.

Letter 5: From Joseph Cabell in Williamsburg to William Cabell in Richmond

Williamsburg, 30th Oct 1806

Dear Brother;

I was not disappointed in the hope that I might get an answer from you by the last mail, to my letter of Sunday last, tho' you only had ten minutes to write in. The old Judge has not been as prompt either in relation to me, or to Mrs. Tucker; he sent her, as usual, a few lines but they were sent off before her letter had reached him. This evening, I suppose, both of us will get something from him, and no doubt an approbation of the proceedings here. Anticipating his consent, I have gone on to the subject of <u>the day</u> [wedding date]*; and in confirmation of my own impressions as to the propriety of the dispatch, I read to Miss Polly, the sentiments* [of] *your last letter. Trembling, blushing, and faultering, she consented to be governed by the opinion of her parents. Mrs. Tucker being still confined to her* *room, and having appeared only once or twice since I came down, and then when there was much company, I have been unable to confer personally with her on this subject. Indeed not a word has yet passed between us respecting the affair. She sent me her consent by her daughter, and I know only thro' the medium of others, that she expresses the most sincere satisfaction, at the proposed union. Yesterday, my old friend John H. Cocke came over to the second day of the Races, and he had a long conference with her [Lelia Tucker] last evening, in which he urged the propriety of yielding to my desire that we should be married about the 20th of Nov'r. Tho' frightened at the thought of giving away her daughter so soon, she confessed the propriety of dispatch; but protested against the event's taking place before the arrival of Mrs. Coalter [Fannie], who cannot conveniently come down till Christmas. This being the opinion of Miss Polly also, I suppose I must yield as calmly as possible to the last prerogative of the sex; but, by Jupiter, I don't know how I shall contrive to worry down the tedious interval. I think of coming up in Saturday's stage. But, I shall not be able to keep myself long in Richmond, before I shall be back again. I will return to spend some days in the beginning of the session of Assembly. Thus shall I be urged to two more trips before the great day arrives. Since my last to you, I have as usual spent my mornings and evenings at the Judge's, where I also frequently breakfast and dine; and the confinement of Mrs. Tucker has given me the advantage of many solitary hours with her daughter. The most unaffected and ardent attachment animates our bosoms; & I sincerely believe that no two young persons were embarked in life, with a more cordial embrace, or with more confident expectations of happiness. I knew comparatively nothing of this lovely girl at the time I left you. She is indeed a gentle spirit; an affectionate, mild, retiring, modest, amiable girl, professing a good natural understanding, much more cultivated than that of the generality of her sex. Her character displays itself in new and amiable lights at every interview. I swear, by the God that made me, that I prefer her to the whole world, and I do not believe that the sun sees in his course a man more truly happy than myself. Could anything be more delightful to a man in my situation, than to be assured, that twelve months ago, this lovely woman declared that, should I ever put it in her power, she would marry me; and that her mother, in being applied to for her consent, observed, that had she hunted the world over she could not have found one to whom she would have given her daughter with more cheerfulness than myself. I burst into a flood of tears & drop my pen in an extasy of joy. Yours most sincerely,*

Joseph C. Cabell

P.S. My love to my Sister, to Nicholas, to Upshaw, Randolph, Gamble, etc.

The central thoughts of this letter need no further explanation. In the postscript, the sister is William's wife Agnes; Nicholas is their young son; Randolph is quite certainly Peyton Randolph, attorney and William & Mary classmate of the Cabells; and Gamble is likely to be John or Robert, brothers of Agnes (*nee* Gamble.) Another new figure merits a full introduction:

John Hartwell Cocke (b. 1780) – Cocke attended William and Mary at the same time as Cabell. They there formed a close friendship based especially upon their shared love of the natural sciences and agriculture. Cocke grew up on the Mount Pleasant estate, sixteen miles as the crow flies from Williamsburg, but on the south side of the James River. In 1802 he married Anne Blaws 'Nancy' Barraud, daughter of Dr. Philip Barraud, a close Williamsburg friend and neighbor of the Tuckers. At the time of this story, the couple were in the lengthy process of leaving the tidewater area for *Bremo,* an estate that Cocke was developing on the upper James. It would put them in the mountainous upper country where the Cabells had long resided.

Cocke's friendship with the Tuckers went back at least as far as Cabell's, and he was much liked by them. He would have been at ease and enjoyed serving as an advocate to Lelia on behalf of Joseph. Furthermore, his wife Nancy had been a friend of Polly (four years younger) from the time of their growing up together as neighbors in Williamsburg.

Letter 6: From Joseph Cabell in Williamsburg
to St. George Tucker in Richmond

Williamsburg, 31ˢᵗ Oct 1806

My dear Sir:

Your favor of 28ᵗʰ inst [instant, i.e., this month] *in
reply to my letter of 26ᵗʰ has been communicated to me by
Mrs. Tucker, and read with all the sensibility due to the
respectable source from which it comes, and the importance and interesting nature of its contents. I thank you
most sincerely and cordially for the friendly and respectful
expressions with which you are pleased to honor me, for
the candor with which you speak on this occasion, and the
conditional consent which you give to my marriage with
your adopted Daughter. The terms on which we have long
lived, and the high degree in which my happiness is now
interested, authorize & require that I should speak, also on
my part, with the utmost frankness & independence. This
I shall do with the more confidence, as I am thoroughly
persuaded, that it is only necessary for us to be mutually
understood, in order to be mutually agreed.*

*I entertain not the smallest doubt of your sincerity,
when you assure me, that there is nothing pointed against
me in particular in the precautions you propose to adopt,
and that they are the result of an affectionate solicitude to
guard, as far as possible, against every future obstacle to
the happiness of Miss Carter. I will be vain enough to say,
moreover, that I believe there is scarcely any young man,*

in whose favor you would dispense with such precautions, sooner than with respect to myself. These remarks will convince you that I enter fully into your motives. I now beg you to do equal justice to mine, in listening calmly & impartially to my objections to your proposals.

In relation to the condition of my Mother's express consent, & the assurance of herself and my other relations that they will receive your Daughter to their arms I have only to observe that they would be entirely superfluous. There is not a shadow of a doubt any choice which I might make would be acceptable to them; and that after all they have heard of your family thro' the medium of myself and others, no connexion could be to them a source of more sincere satisfaction. However, I have already written to my mother on the subject and I hope to hear from her in the course of a week.

In respect to your proposition of a marriage settlement, it places me in a situation truly painful and delicate. Were I to consent, I should do that to which I have ever been opposed; were I to refuse, I might appear to the suspicious to be governed by interested considerations [self-interest]. *I belong to a family whose situation in life has not rendered it necessary for them to pay particular attention to such subjects. But whenever such cases have come within limits of my observation, I have conceived a strong aversion to such a practice. I am perfectly aware, my dear Sir, of the purity or your motives on this occasion; but I beseech you to figure to yourself the feelings with which a young man of spirit and honor ought to be inspired by such a proposition. When viewed abstractedly from your declarations on the subject, does it not argue a distrust of my motives, & of my character? Does it not hold me up in the light of an adventurer, to whom Miss Carter might bestow herself, but not confide her fortune? Does it place the young Lady herself in an elevated point of view, to suppose her able of taking to her bosom a man in whom she could not repose unbounded confidence? Does it not convey the idea that all the advantages of the union are on one side, while nothing is thrown into the opposite scale, and that at the same moment I am devoting myself to your Daughter she reserves a portion of herself from me? Under the trammels of a marriage settlement, I should embark in life without energy of character and with the appearance of a humiliated dependent. There would be an odious and embarrassing separation of interests between me and my wife. I could not change the nature of her property, and wield it to the advantage of our family accordingly as times, circumstances, and views in life might require. My children would become independent of the controul I ought to hold over them. I am profoundly persuaded, respected Sir, that you did not view your proposition in these lights, but I conscientiously believe that such would be the inconveniencies of acceding to it; such the impressions of the public; and these with me were powerful considerations.*

It has been now many years since I had the pleasure of an immediate acquaintance in your family; and Miss Carter's situation as to fortune was as well known to me six years ago as at this moment. Tho' I have been driven, as it were by a tempest, thro' foreign countries for several years past, it has now been five months since my return home. Had Miss Carter's fortune been a governing consideration with me, I certainly might have profited of the opportunity of throwing myself into her company afforded by the fraternal invitations of our friend Henry to meet him in Staunton in the course of the summer. In that case also I should not have arrived in Richmond and have there been preparing to the knowledge of my friends, to set out on a journey to New York, without regard to the time at which she was to pass on to Williamsburg. Had not my acquaintance there formed with her produced my attachment to her, I should probably never again have seen this old City; nor again have beheld Miss Carter till after we both should have been married, and settled in different and distant scenes. It is painful to me to make such remarks; but they are highly proper, when I cast my eye on the latter part of your letter, & there observe, not withstanding what goes before, that you call on to make a settlement of her property on Miss Carter and thereby to give an "unequivocal pledge of honorable & disinterested attachment to your beloved child."

But tho' I am unwilling to be bound in the way proposed, I am convinced, that my own principles afford a

security for the future welfare of Miss Carter, equivalent
& vastly superior to the one suggested. My unbounded
affection for her, my sacred honor, are better guardians
than legal restraints. Should she survive me without off-
spring, the least I could do for her, would be to leave her
the fortune she brought with her: and in every other case
which could occur, I would do all that an affectionate
husband & a man of honor ought to perform. This I
would do voluntarily; and I would provide against accidents by timely measures. There is nothing more certain
in m mind, and indeed proofs have been given, that
my family in such cases would be as far elevated above
ungenerous & illiberal advantages as any other in the
country.

You know but little of me, Sir, if you do not suppose,
that I would now prefer your Daughter, without a cent,
to any other woman on earth, with the Indies at her com-
mand. If you will bestow her on me, I will cherish her
as the wife of my bosom, and there shall be no necessity
for you "to interpose between her and those sad reverses of
fortune, which you have too often observed among ladies
in Virginia." Her interest shall be mine, and mine shall
be hers. I will endeavor to manage our joint fortune to
the best advantage for our mutual happiness, guided by
the advice of our wiser friends; and to none should I look
with more confidence than to yourself and Mrs. Tucker. I
hope that the knowledge you have of me, I trust that the
history of my past life, afford sufficient evidences, that you

may with safety surrender your Daughter to me without any other conditions, than those imposed by donor and by affection. Reflect, I beseech you, Sir, on the objections I have here taken the liberty to state: & believe me, Dear Sir, when I assure you, that they are accompanied by the most respectful sentiments & warmest regard of your devoted friend.

    J. C. Cabell

Need one say any more? Perhaps. The one passage of this letter that calls for some explanation is that in which Cabell seeks to establish that he is not a fortune seeker. If he were, he argues, he would have accepted the earlier invitation of Polly's stepbrother, Henry St. George, to visit him while Polly also was visiting. The gathering place would not have been Henry's humble abode in Winchester, but the home where the family often gathered in the summers, that of his sister Fannie and her husband John Coalter in Staunton. Furthermore, Cabell argues, if attaching himself to Polly for her wealth had been his motive, he would not have planned a trip to New York at that time; he would have chased her to Williamsburg when she returned from the visit with Henry. Were it not for a chance meeting in Richmond that occurred after his return from Europe, six years would have passed since he had seen her, and each would likely have married someone else. Cabell's belabored point: It was not a plot to get Polly's money, but chance or divine intervention that brought them together.

It is time to formally introduce Henry, first mentioned in this letter:

Henry St. George Tucker (b. 1780) – Henry was the oldest of the three sons born to St. George and his first wife, Frances Bland Randolph. Both parents were assiduous about their children's education and studious Henry more than met their expectations. After obtaining his law degree from William & Mary he moved to Winchester in 1803, at the behest of his father, to try to establish a practice. Charles was sent to spend the summer with him in 1804 in the hope that the older stepbrother might inspire the younger by example. It led instead to great frustration for them both. By the time of this story Henry was finding success in both his work and personal life in Winchester, after his difficult early years of disappointment in both.

Cabell was probably unaware at this time of a deeper connection between himself and his friend, revealed by Henry in the following letter written to his father *two years earlier*: Polly had captured his heart, too.

Letter 7: From Henry S. G. Tucker in Winchester to St. George Tucker in Williamsburg[b]

Winchester, 30th Sept 1804

My dear papa,

This letter is the last you will receive from me before you will have returned to the low country. It is a painful reflection that while I am wishing you a pleasant journey to that spot which to my eye possesses more charms than any in the world, I am also meditating the prospect of my being debarred of the gratification of meeting you there as usual this winter. You will be surprised, my dearest friend, my tenderest of fathers, that I should contemplate a longer separation from you, when you do not perceive the imperious necessity which dictates it. But you who so well know me cannot I am convinced suspect me of a coldness & indifference to those pleasures which formed my greatest delight, or of a diminution of that attachment which it is my pride & my first gratification to find only strengthened by time. You will rather attribute it to its proper cause, to a wish to avoid the painful scenes which I passed this last winter, & of which the events of the summer have taught me to expect a repetition. Yes, my dear papa, I at length find the necessity of endeavouring to subdue those feelings which could never be gratified, and to stifle a passion which has ceased to be encouraged even by the smallest ray of hope. Such indeed has for some time been my anxious wish and I have cautiously avoided writing on a subject matter which, I never can think of without pain and which it has become my interest, if possible, to forget. Had [blank space] *preserved to me the conduct she had formerly done or had she even placed me on the footing of a common acquaintance, I might still have felt the delusions of hope & encouraged an expectation of engaging her affections. But the mind, when conscious of being degraded, always makes some energetic effort to regain its level; and when I could not but perceive that her conduct manifested not only her indifference to me as a lover, but perhaps her contempt for me as a man; when the coldness & distance of her manner would not fail on every occasion to embarrass me, & degraded me in the eyes of others; & when from her persisting in the same <u>slighting</u> reserve, I had every reason to believe it the fixed determination of her mind, I felt as if it were a duty to myself to endeavour to reassume at a distance from her that independence which I never could attain in her presence. Hurt, nay stung to the quick while I was at Staunton, I half-formed this resolution which however I communicated to no one, and have since been constantly endeavouring to train my mind to that desirable state which is now my only resort. There was a time when my union with* [blank space] *was the fondest subject of my thoughts & employed my mind even in my dreams. But it has proved indeed but a baseless vision, which hard necessity now forces me to endeavour to forget. I need not assure you, my dear Sir, that this end is not attained. I am not possessed of that volatility which might enable me to*

throw off in a moment that attachment I have once felt.
I can only expect from time & absence a complete cure.
Long reflection has taught me to avoid seeing her again
until I shall be conscious that she no longer possesses the
same power over my heart. Thank God! That my feelings
are sufficiently cool to make this determination. Were I to
spend the winter with her, I should no longer be able to
boast of so much fortitude & calmness; and I should feel
little pleasure in a society where I should every moment
be reminded of my situation & where I should consider
myself as the object of the unavailing <u>pity</u> of those around
me: and where in the name of heaven! can there be a more
degrading and mortifying reflection!!

I appreciate highly the motives which I [illegible]
have alone actuated. If, as I imagine, she has done violence
[illegible: *to my?*] *feelings in assuming a conduct which*
might destroy hopeless passion, she is entitled to and shall
ever possess my warmest gratitude. But it has been a medi-
cine severe & painful in its operation, and which to effect
a cure has produced the acutest anguish. Indeed the readi-
ness with which I can assign such a reason for her conduct
is perhaps a sufficient proof that I am not cured of that
partiality which I felt for her; for perhaps her manner only
expressed that contempt which she really felt for your son
Henry S: G: Tucker

What an outpouring by Henry of his innermost thoughts,
expressing his experience of first love, unrequited love, and the

love of a son for his father. Although Henry left a blank space where the name of the woman he loved would have been written, she was Polly, his stepsister. Other correspondence from this era reveals a wider practice among letter writers of omitting a name from written statements that might later cause them embarrassment or other problems. Given that in their day letters were sometimes passed from hand-to-hand, added to packets with others, or opened by persons other than the recipient, this was a reasonable worry and precaution. In subsequent letters to his father, Henry referred to Polly by name, perhaps knowing that those letters would reach St. George directly.

It should go without saying that in referring to himself as Polly's "lover," Henry meant simply that he loved her. St. George docketed the letter as received by him in October, but did not add his customary note of the date he replied. He likely decided instead to talk to his son in person, and he did. For, contrary to his plan, Henry did join the family in Williamsburg for Christmas, as was their tradition and greatest wish. He wrote the following letter soon after his return to Winchester.

Letter 8: From Henry S.G. Tucker in Winchester
to St. George Tucker in Williamsburg[c]

Winchester, 18th Jan 1805

My dearest papa,

The conversation you had today with Mr. Coalter urges me once more to adopt this method of mentioning to you a subject which I had always been convinced was as painful to you as to myself, and which for that reason I had almost resolved never more to have spoken of to you, until chance or fortune had rendered it more agreeable.

I suggested today to Mr. C. the propriety of turning my thoughts to a life in some measure political, as I had been so unfortunately disappointed in every other prospect. I urged that it was necessary in every situation to have a motive to action, and that I therefore believed it proper to create one to supply the place of that which had hitherto actuated me. Of the propriety of dropping every hope on the subject of marriage I am almost convinced however ag't [against] my will. I know however that the change of Polly's behavior to me has been believed to evince a change in her sentiments. This change however has been produced by my letter to mama, and by the alteration in my own conduct. Were I for a moment to be particular to her, her former coldness would return in a tenfold degree, and I should again feel myself involved in the most embarrassing & perplexing situation. Happily the society of a fine girl has enabled me to be easy (nay more) in the company of

Polly, and in this point of view if in no other I feel much gratified that Maria has spent the Winter with us. I know not how without her aid I should have been able to have preserved my equanimity, or even the appearance of it; or how I should have passed the few weeks I have been with you. Perhaps it may be a strange temper of which I am possessed; but I feel a restraint in the company of one whom I really love, and of whose attachment I have no evidence which prevents familiarity; nay almost begets distance and reserve. There is but one subject that can give interest, and it is one which is ever obtruding itself upon the mind even in the slightest intercourse. When this is forbidden, and when the remotest prospect of success is cut off, nothing is more painful or more perplexing than a particular attention to a woman we love: and there is no greater relief under such circumstances, than the society of any person who can entertain us, and dispel even for a moment the pain of reflection. Such has been nearly my situation. Tho' I give Sister Polly full credit for her exertion in rendering my time less unpleasant than formerly, and tho there is much less reserve between us than hitherto, yet believe me my dear Sir, I feel that reserve, that painful constraint, cannot be subdued either on her part or my own, until I shall cease to love her or she shall begin to reciprocate my affection.

I suppose I need not say my <u>heart</u> is not changed. My judgment indeed has often suggested that it might be happy for me if I could transfer my affections to another.

But however I have wished it I have not yet found it even remotely possible. What then shall I do? Shall I torment or rather pester her with addresses which I am convinced must be fruitless, and may render her really my enemy; Or shall I at length make Ambition (if I may use so strong a term) my mistress, and endeavour to deserve if I cannot possess her, whom I have so fondly loved? For my own part I believe the latter most proper. There is a certain point beyond which, if one goes, he must incur contempt & hatred. I believe I have at least attained that point, & nothing but a clear conviction of propriety, can induce me again to renew the subject. If I ever should believe that circumstances had so far changed as to justify a hope relative to it, no situation could prevent my declaring the continuance of my love. But until that happens, such an avowal shall never proceed from me either mediately or immediately however I might wish to be convinced that "time in vain endeavours to free the heart from affection's [illegible] chain."

To the bar then, entirely, or to the assembly & the [bar] together, my attention ought now therefore to be wholly turned. How far it may be proper to pursue both together may perhaps be the subject of another letter.

After sitting up three nights I fear I have not written very connectedly or correctly. It may therefore happen that I have expressed ideas, I did not intend.

Your Son affectionately,
Henry S:G: Tucker

*I shall leave you to determine whether to show this letter
to my best of mothers. You know I would conceal from her
nothing save what my affection for her would prompt me
to hide.*

The Maria who was also a guest at the Tucker home remains
unknown, though she was probably a cousin. Her presence
helped Henry, but he continued to grapple with both his unrequited love and his struggle to become a success in his own eyes
and those of his parents. Soon after his return to Winchester,
he seriously considered running for office as a member of the
Virginia Assembly and conveyed the idea to his father, through
a letter carried to Williamsburg by his brother-in-law John
Coalter. We do not have St. George Tucker's letter to Henry in
reply, but we do have Henry's response to it.

Letter 9: From Henry S.G. Tucker in Winchester
to St. George Tucker in Williamsburg

Winchester, 10ᵗʰ Feb. 1805

My dearest papa,

I have deferred writing to you until this hour, that I might have more leisure to answer your letter which was delivered me by Mr. Coalter.

I own I was surprised, my dear Sir, at the anxiety which you expressed relative to Mr. Coalter's communication to you, and to the letter which I wrote you. In what have I justified a want of confidence in my implicit obedience to your will, however our opinions might differ? What reason have I ever given you to believe that I would not abandon the most favorite scheme if it did not meet with your unqualified approbation? Can the prospect of my independence make an alteration in my sentiments? Because I no longer need your aid, or because I may sanguinely hope so, shall I forget that you are my father and that some regard is due to the happiness of one who has cherished me with <u>more</u> than paternal affection? – I, whose greatest pleasure has ever been to make you happy on my account, and whose prospects now seem to have that end alone? Thank God! I still have it; and may it never cease to animate me, since it must guide me to virtue & real honour!

Whatever uneasiness you may have had on this subject, for the present at least may cease. The idea of going to the assembly was first prompted by the expectation that one of our present members would resign. That however will not be the case so that it is needless to say any thing in answer to your [illegible: *words?*] *on that subject. There is another* [subject] *which I fear never will cease to be interesting to me, and the manner in which you mention it gave me for a moment extreme concern. You say, "If your resolution with respect to matrimony be the result of any change in your mind either with regard to the <u>object</u> or the <u>state</u>, I must consider it precipitate and unfortunate." Have you then, my dearest Sir, had a doubt of the sincerity of my repeated assurances that my heart was unchanged? I confess that from the bottom of my soul I wish it were changed, as I feel a painful conviction that I have no reason to expect a favourable alteration of circumstances. I wish I were capable of throwing off a passion which seems only calculated to disquiet me. But I find it impossible. It seems almost grafted in my nature. Business may dispel reflection, company may cheer me, but in retirement, at those moments when the most endearing connection is the most inestimable, I cannot help recurring to those scenes which I have left, and entertaining those wishes which are now scarcely rational. Even company has in some measure lost its efficacy. Last winter I found myself much more cheerful in society than at present. There is a tedium, a weariness, a disgust that seems to overwhelm me when I enter a numerous company. I have resorted to a new plan: Close confinement to my pen* [writing] *till I am actually fatigued – and then I seek for somebody who* *will talk to me of W_ g* [Williamsburg]. *This does not argue a change in my affections. I am convinced they are if possible warmer than ever. The amiable, the gentle, the enchanting conduct of polly* [lowercase 'p' in the original] *during the winter, has bound me if possible more than ever to her. It is from this conviction that I may have felt and expressed some hasty sentiment on the subject of marriage. Not that I feel a prejudice ag't* [against] *that state which I have ever regarded as the most happy, but because without love, it is miserable, and I have no love to bestow on more than one person. And I repeat it, my dearest father, I have already gone perhaps too far: to go farther would degrade me in polly's eyes unless she loved me; till then I would not by word or action give her reason to believe I was still so far a slave to passion, as to do any thing she would think improper. She cannot doubt my affection and there is not therefore any reason for irritating her with an assurance of it. But should the moment ever arrive when I may reasonably believe her sentiments are more favourable I should seize with avidity any opportunity of convincing her of my constancy and reaping the reward of it.*

You will of course show this letter to mama. Assure her that I love her more dearly than ever, as every day furnishes fresh proofs of her tenderness to me. My best love to all your fire side. I hope I shall soon hear some account of you. Your circle [of guests] *I presume is by this time much contracted.*

Your affect. Son
Henry S.G. Tucker

It is possible Mr. Peyton will deliver this. As I have uniformly received the most pointed attention from his friends here, I must take the liberty of recommending him to your civilities while he is in W_ g.

Henry soon prevailed over his challenges in both work and love. After many setbacks, his law practice began to grow; and he met another young woman who won his heart. In September of 1806 he married Ann Evelina Hunter, daughter of Moses Hunter, clerk of the court of Berkeley County. Thus when Henry invited Cabell to visit him, it was for Cabell to join with Polly in meeting his new wife for the first time.

Returning to the present, with Cabell's intrepid countering letter [No. 6] on its way to St. George in Richmond, a letter written to him also arrived at the capital – from his mother. The spelling and punctuation are hers.

Letter 10: From Hannah Cabell in Warminster to Joseph Cabell in Richmond

Ly [Liberty] *Hall, 31ˢᵗ Oct 1806*

Dear Joe,

Yours of 26ᵗʰ Instant came to hand this day, and an opportunity offering by a Mr. Hunley [to carry it to Richmond] *I have embraced it.*

You wish my approbation to marry my dear Son, the world is before you and I rely on your own judgement to please your self and in doing so you will please me. no doubt but you have already considered that it is the most important event of your life but have you considered where you are to put her, you have no house of your own, you also know that in a few weeks I shall have none to make her welcome in. I could wish this could have hapened a little sooner that I might at least have had the pleasure of entertaining for once in my Own house. I have no doubt but I shall be pleased with her, Agnes speaks highly of her, whose opinion and judgement I put great Confidence in. your brother wrote me on the subject last week Landon hapned here a few days after and as I know he was in all your secrets I showed him the letter, and for the same reasons I have inclosed it to the Doctor, I expect him do [due] *in a few days, the Old gentleman is from home. tell Billy* [William Cabell] *I have not time to write him at present but I shall want a large trunk 4 or 5 feet long. my white family are well but we have an Obstanate Billious fever among the negroes, why will you forget your*

Old friends, you have said nothing about Mrs. Tazewell,
Should you see her give my love to her. every boddy but my
self is in bed good night from your affectionate Mother
        HC Cabell

PS Nichs [Nicholas] *and Peggy laugh heartily at present*
sittuation and wish much to see you and your intended
Lady.

Hannah's sons "Joe" and "Billy" clearly remained subject to both her love and scoldings. The unnamed doctor is Dr. William Hare. Hannah, a widow since 1803, was in the midst of leaving her home, Liberty Hall, for his home Harewood, in nearby Amherst County. Hare's wife Elizabeth, Hannah's daughter, died in 1802 and Hannah had helped ever since in caring for her orphaned granddaughters. Now she was moving to Harewood in order to be with the girls full time. Hare, a great favorite of all in the Cabell family, and always referred to simply as "the Doctor," was at this time in Richmond, preparing for the upcoming legislative session as the state senator from Amherst County.

Letter 11: From Joseph Cabell in Williamsburg
to William Cabell in Richmond

Williamsburg, 1ˢᵗ Nov 1806

Dear Brother,

I enclose for your perusal these two letters [Nos. 4 &
6] *which have passed between Judge Tucker and myself,
on the subject of my proposed marriage. You find that
the hint in your last* [missing letter] *was not superfluous, and that I have acted in conformity; tho' it only
gave new vigor to my own impulse on that subject. I
confess I have been much disappointed in the conduct of
the Judge, and should be irritated were he to persevere. I
had even been so confident as to hope that, like yourself,
he would have sent me an answer by the next mail after
that which conveyed him mine: but I was certain of one
on Thursday evening. I had dropped my last to you into
the office, only a half hour before the stage arrived that
evening. You may suppose that my feelings were a little
chilled, when on the opening of the mail, I could find
no other letter, than your own: tho' I repeatedly asked,
if there was not another. As my friend Cocke & myself
walked to Mr. Bassetts' to dinner, and I expressed much
surprise & anxiety at not getting some thing from the
Judge, C. remarked to me, "You know Tucker's intrin-
sic merit as well as myself; but perhaps you have yet to
learn, that he is in some things an odd kind of man; and
I should not be surprized, if he were to come forward*

with propositions on this occasion which might be disagreeable to your feelings." I promptly replied that such conduct had a strong squinting towards what I knew he alluded to, and should such attempts be made, I should certainly resist them. He dropped the subject at the door, hoping that Mr. T. may have sent his reply under cover to Mrs. T., and that I should get it in the evening. While the bottle was going round, & just after the cloth had been removed, I was told that a servant wished to see me at the door. On retiring I met one of Mr. Tucker's servants, with the enclosed letter for me from the Judge, under the cover from Mrs. Tucker. I retired to the corner of the House, and read it with much agitation; – collected myself, returned, and gave Mr. Wirt the wink to walk out with me: when I addressed him in the style of my reply to Mr. Tucker, he approved highly of my opinions & feelings on the occasion. He advised me to go immediately and convince the young lady of the purity of my motives, in opposing such wishes on the part of her parents; then to write to or converse with her Mother; and finally to give my reasons to the Judge himself. He returned and sent out Mr. Cocke, who walked with me up to Mr. Tucker's & approved of the course I was taking, as I stated it to him on the way. On arriving we found an acquaintance of the family sitting with Miss Carter, and begged a private interview with her. As soon as I was alone I depicted to her the nature of my feelings on reading her Father's letter. Her conduct was noble, & all that

*I could desire. In a flood of tears, she pressed my hand &
said, "Sir, I have read the letter, but I know nothing, &
think nothing, of such matters. Your heart, is all that I
desire." Pressing her to my bosom, "Beloved girl," replied
I, "you possess it already, and all that I ask in return is
your own." This was truly a scene of most exquisite tenderness. On this occasion, as well on many others, this
lovely girl has consecrated herself in my affections. She
told me that her Mother had merely followed the advice
of her Father, and that she would see that she should
retract her letter that very evening. Cocke had some conversation with Mrs. T, who seemed disposed to do every
thing that was right. Next morning I wrote an answer to
Mr. Tucker, of which I send you the enclosed copy, and
Mr. C [Cocke] showed it to Mrs. T, in her chamber. He
returned with much emotion, & taking me by the hand,
congratulated me on the removal of every difficulty, at
least in Williamsburg, and assured me that he believed
the Judge himself would be perfectly satisfied. Mrs. T.
he said, was extremely affected on reading my letter, &
appeared to be strongly impressed with the impropriety of
her husband's demand. She had never wished any thing
more herself than a provision, were it voluntary on my
part, against the possible cases alluded to; & she promised
to enclose my letter to the Judge, with an approbation of
all its contents, and request him to say nothing more on
the subject. This she did last evening, & her daughter
tells me, that she observed to him, that it should be the*

effort of her life <u>to merit my esteem</u>. Herself and Colonel Skipwith & family appear delighted at the connexion, & I doubt not that the Judge himself has only made a little aristocratic parade on the occasion, in order to appear not to give way too easily on so interesting a subject. Should he resist, it will be in vain; for the girl is mine, by all thirty thousand gods of the Romans. No two lovers felt as we do, ever since the days of Pyramus & Thisbe. When I [Torn: *cast?*] *my eyes around me, I ask where is the man so happy as myself.* [Torn: *God? Heaven?*] *seems to be repaying me for whole years of affliction. I stand, as it were, on the gilded summit of a lofty mountain, and look down with security on the troubled waters thro' which I have waded. Great Governor of the Universe, I bow before you, & sink into silent & grateful admiration.*

    J.C. Cabell

P.S. All this is confidential; you may shew it to my Sister & Upshaw but under the most solemn injunctions of secrecy.

The home of Burwell Bassett, Jr. was the grandest of any in this account. In 1794 he had purchased two lots on Francis Street near the Capitol. These were landscaped as the formal entranceway to his home, now known as Bassett Hall, set back from the street on the adjoining plantation. A brick mansion, gardens, stables, and other outbuildings greeted its visitors. Bassett was well known to the Cabells and many others, having long served as a state Senator and (since 1805) a member of Congress. Bassett's father (Burwell, Sr.) was a brother-in-law of George Washington, who often visited the family home, Eltham, in New Kent County.

Two other individuals mentioned in this letter deserve formal introductions:

Col. Henry Skipwith (b. 1751) – Henry was Lelia's uncle, her father's brother. A veteran of the Revolution, he was also a brother-in-law of Thomas Jefferson, both men having married daughters of John Wayles. Skipwith first lived with Ann (*neé* Wayles) in Cumberland County, where they built their home, Hors du Monde. Following Ann's death in 1798, he married Elizabeth Byrd and moved with her to Williamsburg around 1801. They lived in Wythe House, a brick mansion across the Palace Green from the Tucker house, which Skipwith purchased from George Wythe, first professor of law at William & Mary. "Uncle Henry" was full of fun and energy, and was especially liked by Charles.

William Wirt (b. 1772) – Born and schooled in Maryland, in 1795 Wirt began his career in law in Virginia. After the death of his first wife in 1799 he moved from their home near Charlottesville to Richmond. There he met and married in 1802 Elizabeth Gamble, the sister of William Cabell's wife Agnes. They moved to Norfolk but, by the time of this story, had returned to Richmond where Wirt set up a private law practice. He there earned a reputation both as an eloquent courtroom orator and author. His well-received, fictional "Letters of the British Spy" were first published in the *Virginia Argus*, a weekly newspaper, and then in book form in 1805. His relationship with the Cabells was that of an intimate friend and relative.

Cabell acted in accord with both that intimacy and his pensive nature by prompting Wirt to leave the table at Bassett Hall for a private chat. He was upset by the position taken by St. George in his letter and wanted Wirt's opinion on the merits of both his reaction and intended response. He then talked the same matters through with his friend Cocke during their walk back to the Tucker house. Had other friends been within reach their views too would have been sought. As it was, the two friends at hand gave Cabell just the endorsement he needed. He was a very happy and very anxious young man, and now wanted to learn what his decisive older brother thought of it all. Accordingly he sent two letters to William, the first being a customary matter of courtesy.

Letter 12: From Joseph Cabell in Williamsburg to William Cabell in Richmond

Williamsburg, 1ˢᵗ Nov 1806

Dear Brother;

Col. Skipwith, of this city, being on the eve of an excursion of some weeks to the vicinity of Petersburg, and proposing to pass thro' Richmond on his way, I have begged the favor of him to permit me to introduce him to your acquaintance & attention, during his short stay in the latter place. He is already too well known to you as Col. Skipwith of Cumberland to require any further introduction by me. You will recollect that I have often remarked to you, that the House of Mrs. Dunbar, now Mrs. Skipwith, was the scene of some of my most delightful hours, during my early stay at the College; and since my late arrival here, I have received the most obliging and friendly attentions from Col. Skipwith & his Lady. I therefore beg you to receive Col. Skipwith in a style suited to such distinguished claims to your regard.

Your affectionate brother,
Joseph C. Cabell

Hospitality to travelers was a central value and practice of the Virginia gentry. Here Cabell was carrying out the most familiar and regular of duties, writing a letter of introduction for someone on his way to a place where he had few, if any, connections of his own. William would be prepared to feed and provide a room for Uncle Henry, if need be.

Letter 13: From Joseph Cabell in Williamsburg to William Cabell in Richmond

Williamsburg, 3rd Nov 1806

Dear Brother,

By the stage which went up on Sunday, I sent you a packet, which before this you have probably perused. As nothing in particular has since occurred, I write at present only to inform you that things are in statu quo. On Wednesday I look for an answer from Mr. Tucker, which, waving all hopes and fears, I expect will be favorable to my wishes. Mrs. T. has great influence over him, and is now on my side unquestionably. Besides, I am satisfied that they would have suffered matters to proceed to such lengths, if they had ever been determined to halt on such untenable ground. I shewed Mr. Wirt the copy of my reply to Mr. Tucker, which he approved very highly, and considered unanswerable. I hope you will equally approve of it. Should the Judge come over [agree with me], *we shall probably be married at Christmas. You & my Sister* [Agnes], *Doctor Hare, & many other friends will of course be here. I now am only awaiting Mr. T's answer; should it be favorable, and arrive on Wednesday, I will come up by Thursday's or Saturday's stage. On my arrival, we will talk over the matter of my going up the country with you, of which I have thoughts at the present; tho' that trip, and the opening of the session of Assembly, I fear, would keep me too long absent from Williamsburg. I will then also answer your*

*questions respecting my domestic affairs up the country;
and I will consult with you as to the propriety of my offering for Amherst in the Spring, or any other course which I
ought to take. Mrs. T. has requested me thro' the medium
of her daughter to remain here as long as possible after we
shall have married, and it is tolerably well understood, that
we shall not leave them at least till next summer, except on
a visit to you during the winter. It seems to be the desire
of them both, that we should live in Richmond, in order
that they may frequently see each other, & for Miss Polly to
have the society of Mrs. Randolph & other friends there,
to whom she is ardently attached: but on this subject they
appear as accommodating as myself; & should my views
direct themselves toward Congress, and it become prudent
on that account for me to establish a residence in part in
our district above, I believe they would not object. Wherever
I may reside, I must prepare a house suited to the occa-
sional reception of Mrs. T. & the Judge, for no doubt she
would wish to be as much with us as possible; and should
we perchance fix in the upper country, our house would
of course become in a great measure the summertime residence of the family. But I am sure they would prefer our
living in Richmond. It would also be agreeable to me, and
more suited to all my views & propensities in life, except
that Lewis Harvie is already looking forward and paving
the way to that district in Congress. Should we determine
on the propriety of my taking that ground permanently
at once, I should doubt whether I ought not to offer for*

the Council at the next session of Assembly, prepare myself for practising the law gradually, frequent the surrounding county courts, for a year or two, and then bid defiance to any rival whatever. Or availing myself of the presence of yourself & family in Richmond, to shade the boldness of the stand, I might in a little time represent the city or county, in conjunction with the rest of the former plan; giving up the project of being a councilor. This would admit of a longer stay here, & more latitude of movement. You will think of these matters by the time I come up. In reply to the family here as to my future residence, I have said, that after our union we would determine on a fair view of our situation, and should that admit of our residing in Richmond, I should be happy to do so, unless political views might lead me to the upper country. But I have frankly told them that my own fortune would not admit of our residing there; and I communicated to Mrs. T a general view of my little patrimony thro' Mr. Cocke, the day on which he gave her my letter, and at the same time, that she thro' him sent me an account of her Daughter's fortune. Mrs. T's conduct in this affair has been dignified & highly pleasing to me. Should my friend the judge not come athwart me again with some left-handed proposition, I may safely say that no man ever glided into the gentle vale of matrimony with better prospects of success. My agitated dreary soul longs for the pleasures of domestic retirement. I have seen enough of the world to know whither to look for the most solid enjoyments of which life is susceptible.

I need not enjoin your confidence as to such letters as these. You would do [torn: well?] to be cautious how you write up the country <u>on a certain subject</u> [torn: if there?] be much babbling, I fear, after all, on that head; than which nothing will be more grating to my feelings. Upshaw promised me most sacredly never to mention what passed between us in Richmond. Perhaps it would be prudent to strengthen, by repeating, that impression on his mind. I fear misconstruction only: my motives throughout have been unsullied: but the best way to make them appear indubitably so, even to the suspicious, would be a dignified silence, to all but intimate friends.

Tell my Sister that Miss Polly says she already feels for her the affection of a sister; and that her only wish is to be as much beloved by my relations, as they are by herself. To day I dine with Mr. Wirt at the Rawleigh.

Yours affectionately,
Joseph C. Cabell

Cabell's restless mind churned on. Not only had he obtained Wirt's review of his written reply to St. George, but he had then sent a full copy of it to William for his opinion. In addition, we see that he sought his brother's thoughts on every other decision he then faced, from whether to make a quick visit home, to where to live after marriage, to whether or not to run for office, and, if so, which one? As governor and with his extensive political connections, William's view on the latter matters would be hard for Joseph to question.

But what had Cabell said in Richmond that now made him so gravely worried that it be repeated? Was it simply that there be no leaks of his interest in running for some office, or something very personal? Had he earlier told others why he was not attracted by Polly before completely changing his mind? Whatever he wished kept secret was perfectly clear to William, but hardly at all to us. From much else said in the letter, including his disclosure to Lelia that his own fortune was insufficient to purchase a home in Richmond, it may be that he had earlier said in company that marriage to Polly would make him a rich man. Were *that* remark, though true, to be misconstrued, Cabell would rightly have feared that both his case and his honor would be all but sunk with St. George. His motives for marriage would not appear "unsullied."

He soon received the reply from the judge that he was so anxiously awaiting.

Letter 14: From St. George Tucker in Richmond to Joseph Cabell in Williamsburg

Richmond, 3ʳᵈ Nov 1806

My dear Sir,

I hasten to reply to your favor of the 31ˢᵗ ult. [ultimate, last month], *this day received; and shall do it with the same Candour that prompted my former Letter, and which evidently pervades your answer to it.*

Permit me to assure you most solemnly & unequivocally that there is not in the world a man in whose honour, liberality, & disinterested attachment to the Child of my affections, I could, or should repose a more unbounded confidence than in yours; nor one to whom a more sincere esteem and friendship founded upon a long acquaintance, and strengthened by the knowledge of your attachment to my dear Child, exists in my breast. Consequently I cannot but regret that you should have put upon a particular expression in my Letter a sense different from that which I intended, or conceived it possible for you to adopt. Personal considerations being therefore entirely out of the Question, let me be permitted to answer you as if we were discussing a point where feeling also is out of the question.--Premising, however, that a perfect Confidence in the Honour and disinterested attachment of the parties, to each other, forms the Basis (it may be supposed) of all marriages; and that recourse in such Cases is had to Settlements only to guard against unforeseen accidents & events. But before I proceed, permit me to say a few words on the subject of

Feeling. It happened to myself that the father of my first wife, knowing she possessed a fortune at her own disposal, made the same proposition to me that I have done to you. Far from feeling myself hurt at the proposal, I acceded to it cheerfully, and a Settlement actually took place. Again, when Mr. Coalter addressed my Daughter I made to him the same proposition, as to you, precisely, as far as I can recollect: there Was not, nor is there a man in the universe a man [repeated in original] *whom I knew better, esteemed more, or would have preferred as the husband of my Daughter. Mr. Coalter hesitated not to accede to it: and having myself given, in my own case, and received from him in the case of my daughter, "such an unequivocal pledge of honourable and disinterested attachment," I hesitated not to propose you, with a confidence, arising from Esteem, and not from distrust: My disappointment consequently was commensurate with my Expectations. My proposal, therefore, originating in a Sense of Duty, and propriety, founded on experience and observation, solely with a view to guard against accidents and Events beyond my present foresight, I must beg leave to say, that no arguments drawn merely from Feelings which I have myself encountered, and cheerfully submitted to, are sufficient to counterbalance in my mind the weighty reasons which have induced my Conduct.*

Permit me to reply to another observation in your Letter. You say that in Case of Settlement "you could not change the nature of her property and wield it to the advantage of your family, as times, circumstances, and views in Life might require." I confess, my dear Sir, that I have seen the attempt to meliorate a good fortune in Lands & Slaves, so often attended with utter ruin to the owner, that it is among my strongest reasons for preserving my Childs Estate to her & her Children in its present State. The advantages & disadvantages of transmutation of property in this Country are frequently incalculable; with this Exception, that the disadvantages are often felt through Life, while the advantages (if any) are reserved for remote posterity. I could without difficulty name instances which must carry conviction in a moment.

Again you say, "your Children would become independent of the controul you ought to hold over them." – No, my dear Sir, I cannot persuade myself you have any thing of this sort fear. What controul had I ever, over the first Children of both my wives? None, whatsoever, in point of interest: but in point of affectionate deference, and filial respect, I might say with truth, my own Children never paid me more.

And now, my dear Sir, permit me to state a few of those considerations which have long since determined [me] to adopt the Course I have, whenever the Occasion might require.

The inequality and injustice of our laws in respect to females forms one of the principal reasons for it.

A woman possessing a fortune in Lands, Slaves, & Money, marries. The instant she does so, her Slaves and Money are exclusively her Husbands. If indebted, they go to the payment of his debts, without reserve. If he dies indebted, the whole may be taken to pay his debts; she can have no portion but of the surplus. Of that surplus, however small, she has but one third, if it be in money: if it be of Slaves, she has only the <u>use of one third</u>, <u>for her life only</u>, subject to <u>forfeiture</u> if she carries any of them out of the State. If disposed to marry again she has nothing for her future Children, but her Lands. Even these, (according to every day's practice in Virginia) are only nominally her own: For where is the wife in Virginia that ever refused to put her hand to a Deed conveying away her whole Estate, and then with tears in her eyes, and a breaking heart, going into Court, and acknowledging she did it freely, & without Coercion? I have received too many such acknowledgements & admitted too many such Deeds to record, not to have ejaculated, inwardly, an execration of the Laws which permitted a poor meek woman to be so ruined.

But it may be said, prudence & a will obviate these objections. They may — But how many are there who die involved; or if not involved, who die intestate? And then, the poor wife must pack up with a mere pittance of what was once, & ought still to be her own. It is to save the necessity of keeping Prudence always upon the look out, and to guard against dying intestate that I have proposed that you should settle upon my Child, what is hers. I have asked nothing more: though certainly I conceive that Reciprocity should dictate such an interest in your Estate, in Case of surviving you, as the Law would give her. But even in that case the Law is unequal: as Tenant by the

Curtesy the husband surviving his wife by whom he has had a child enjoys the whole of her Estate during life; she must be contented with one third of his.

Again, my dear Sir, let me recall your attention to my situation: not a natural, but an adopted father, with all the feelings of the natural father, superadded to the responsibility of disposing properly of the Child of another Man, possessing an Estate derived from him; without consulting the wishes or Opinions of her relations, to whom in certain Events the laws might give her property. Can you conceive, my dear Sir, that my feelings, also, are interested, in such a situation? And can you wish that I should sacrifice not only these feelings, but my Judgment, and a long and thoroughly weighed resolution, in which you, certainly were never expected to be comprehended. I repeat it, my dear Sir, my proposal as it relates to yourself has nothing personal: and I beg you to believe my only inducement to insist on it is to guard against unforeseen Accidents and Events, my only object being to secure to our Child in Case of surviving you, the same Independence in regard to the Quantity, and nature of her Estate, that she now enjoys; that her Children by any future marriage may participate equally with any others; & that she may be, as far as I am able to place her, beyond the reach of adverse fortune; I confess I feel some surprise as well as regret at your repugnance to a proposal, by accepting which you would have enabled me to obey the warmest impulse of My heart, by uniting your hands, and seeing you happy in each other. I hesitate not, frankly to avow my ardent wish to do so; and I flatter myself that the

next Letter I receive from you will remove the only obstacle that remains to my fullest, and most cordial Consent to your union. In the mean time believe me with the most sincere esteem and regard, most truly your friend
    S: G: Tucker

Thus Cabell did not receive the reply for which he had longed, "waving all hopes and fears." Rather, the judge held firm to his sense of duty to Polly, and went to great lengths to convey that it implied no distrust of Joseph. The unfairness of the law in its treatment of the property brought by a woman to her marriage was not at issue between the two men. Rather, they disagreed over what should be done in light of that unfairness. Cabell had appealed to his love and judgment as the means to overcome the shortcomings of the law. St. George Tucker preferred a document. The next letter from William Cabell, conveying his point of view, probably reached his brother the next day.

Letter 15: From William Cabell in Richmond
to Joseph Cabell in Williamsburg

Richmond, 4ᵗʰ Nov 1806

Dear Brother,

I received your packet [containing letters 3 & 5, not 13] *on Sunday night the contents of which very much surprised me. At the time I gave you the hint in my letter* [not found] *last week it was not as much that I expected any such proposition, as that I wanted an opportunity to introduce the <u>delicate</u> figure of the stone horse. I was pleased with your reply, and think you have come up to my simile precisely. You seem to have considered the subject very correctly & I hope you will not relinquish <u>an</u> <u>inch</u> of the ground you have taken. I would accede to no modification of the terms of any kind. I would not bind myself to leave a single cent in this that or any other way. I am opposed to marriage settlements on principle, except in particular circumstances. They are not only wrong in principle, but they are <u>degrading</u> in the estimation of fellow citizens. And whatever my attachment to any woman might be, I would renounce her I would renounce an angel, if I could only procure her by submitting to terms which are contrary to principle, & degrading & humiliating in the estimation of myself and others. I hope Mr. Tucker has been influenced only by his paternal anxiety for Miss Carter. But I had rather he had manifested it in some other mode. Should he persevere, I hope you will not be softened by your affection* *for Miss Carter into a forgetfulness of what you owe your friends and your own character. I should rather you be deprived of the use of both hands than that you should put either of them to an instrument that would seal your shame. I hope however he will withdraw his condition. He did not get Mrs. Tucker's letter till Monday, for I saw him about 12 o'clock coming from the office, and on my enquiry after Mrs. Tucker's health, he said he had not had time to read it. I presume he will answer your letter to night. Let me know by the return of the mail the purport of his answer if you give me five words only. I called to see him the other morning & found him very busy preparing for Court. It was two mornings before I received your letter. Not suspecting that he was raising any difficulties, I wondered he did not mention the subject. Mrs. P. [Peyton] Randolph told me this morning that he had informed her he wanted to do it but could not bring it about. She speaks of the event as if settled, & says Mr. Tucker is much pleased by the match. She seems perfectly unacquainted with the subject of his letter. I pretended that you had not heard from him when you last wrote to me.*

Dr. Hare says wonders will never cease. He had taken up the idea that I was the most fickle man in the world; but he says you are my own dear brother. He had not heard of the state of the negotiation when he wrote, but I had told him all about it, except Mr. Tucker's letter. When Landon Cabell heard of it, "two to one" says he, "the young traveller trips up [upon?] the heels of the fair goddess."

Col. Skipwith called here to day & left yours [letter]
[torn: *& I*] *am sorry that neither Agnes nor myself was
at home. But I shall seek him out tomorrow, & I hope he
will not leave town before I shall have an opportunity to
return some of his or rather his lady's civilities to you. Have
you ever got a letter from Coles since you determined on
your present plan of operations? When will you be up? Col.
Gamble has been very ill, but is now getting well again.*

*If I had not shown your last letter to Agnes, I should
have committed a terrible blunder, for I should have sent
to Judge Tucker the copy of the letter which you sent for my
perusal, not attending to the circumstance of your having
sent it to Mrs. Tucker to be forwarded. You had better get
married as soon as possible, for you afford conversation for
the whole town and will continue to do so until the affair
is brot to a close. Agnes & the colonel (I mean Nicholas)
send their love to you.*

Yours, etc. W H Cabell

As ever, Joseph was left in no doubt about where his brother
stood. The contrasting characters of the two men could not be
better drawn. Where Joseph would question, William would
act. Where Joseph would offer his ideas with great deliberation
and a host of reasons, William would proclaim his with excla-
mation points and underlining. Where Joseph would weigh
every decision from every angle, seek the opinions of others,
and then continue to agonize over it when taken, William
would reach a quick conclusion, act on it, and be ready to face

any criticism. His delight in advising, chiding, and teasing his younger brother on this occasion is obvious. It also testifies to their bond of brotherly love.

We also receive in this letter, via the comment of Dr. Hare, a gleeful confirmation that "fickle" Joseph had indeed reversed course with regard to his interest in Polly, and had thereby provided sport for his entire circle of friends. Not only that, but (and one may need to read the following twice): had William not shown to Agnes *the copy* of Joseph's letter to St. George, which Joseph had sent to him (in order to get his opinion), then William, under the impression that the letter he had received was *the original* to be read by him and then *delivered* to St. George, would have done just that. St. George would thereby have received *two* copies of the same letter, which would be surprising enough. But worse, William's previous pretending to St. George that he was unaware of Joseph's present mission would have been undone in an instant! Agnes saved the day by explaining to William that his was a *copy* of the letter to be *kept*, and kept secret.

No wonder the whole family was so entertained by Joseph's progress in "the world of gallantry." But, in contrast to all the laughter in Richmond, Joseph was characteristically as serious and worried as ever in Williamsburg. In theatrical terms, he saw himself in the midst of a tragedy, not a comedy.

Letter 16: From Joseph Cabell in Williamsburg to William Cabell in Richmond

Williamsburg, 5ᵗʰ Oct 1806

Dear Brother,

Yours of yesterday has come to hand, & I write a hasty reply, in obedience to your request, to let you know how matters now stand. Judge Tucker has sent me a long reply, in friendly terms, answering my letter in all its parts, & adhering to his own terms. It came under cover [was addressed] *to Mrs. Tucker, at whose house I now am, & whence I now write you. I have had some conversations with Polly alone, who still avows the most perfect confidence in me, but trembles at the idea of opposing the will her Father. To Mrs. Tucker separately I have expressed my sentiments on the occasion: who, with symptoms of strong embarrassment, declares that it is a condition on which she would not insist if she stood alone, but says she knows not how to oppose the opinion of Mr. Tucker, in an affair which so intimately concerns the happiness of her Daughter, to whom he has been so good a Father. Thus I stand; after a short conversation, to which Judge Nelson has put a stop by coming in. We both lodged here last night; and shall again to-night; by the warm invitation of Mrs. Tucker he is supposed to know nothing of the matter. It is a secret here, & ought certainly remain so. I keep Mr. T.'s letter to shew to Mr. Wirt to-morrow, by whose opinion I shall in this matter be very much guided. I shall*

hold off & come away to Richmond on Saturday, unless advised to the contrary. It now becomes a question, how far I ought to sacrifice my own feelings to the harmony which ought to exist between me & the Judge in future. My own opinion remains the same, & unquestionably I shall not yield without the most evident necessity. You will probably see me Saturday evening. In the interim hold a silent & dignified course at Richmond. My love to my Sister. Yours affectionately,
  Joseph C. Cabell

As one would expect, Cabell remained grave and worried, and saw nothing to laugh about in his situation; hence, his closing appeal for discretion and dignity on the part of the family. William's next letter, without prompting, complied with his younger brother's wish for more analysis and less levity.

Letter 17: From William Cabell in Richmond to Joseph Cabell in Williamsburg

Richmond, 6ᵗʰ Nov 1806

Dear Brother,

Owing to some derangement in the Post office in consequence of changing from the Summer to the Winter Establishment, there was no mail on Tuesday night from Williamsburg, and therefore I was much disappointed in not getting a letter – However I could not have gotten the information I wished with respect to the Judge's answer, as I presume it was not sent before yesterdays mail. I presume altho' you had not many minutes to write last night, that you will follow my example, and give me the substance of the communication. If Mrs. Tucker has heartily withdrawn her assent to the condition made by Him, as you were induced to believe, there can be no doubt but that he will ultimately yield. But it will not be with as much ease as you suspect. You know he is a man of a lofty spirit, & he will not like to come down so readily – altho' he may do so after he has had an opportunity of reflecting & of seeing that the wishes of his family are against him – I dined yesterday with him and a large party at Mr. Randolph's – old Judge Lyons in the course of one of his long stories at table, observed that Miss Carter was going to be married. The observation [was] made in such a way as not to require that any person should make any reply, & the conversation went on, as if it had not been made. Peyton Randolph who sat next to me, told me his eye was fixed on Mr. Tucker to see what effect the observation would have, & saw that he did not like it – You know his delicacy & the tenderness of his feelings, and I presume therefore that such an observation could not be otherwise than unpleasant – He will dine with me tomorrow, with the other Judges. Col. Skipwith left town yesterday, but not before I had called twice to see him, without finding him in. I will try & see him on his return –

I send you mother's letter, which I opened, knowing it to be from her. Her answer is just such as I expected, except that I did suppose she would have paid more regard to my evidence of the merit of her intended daughter. She notices what Agnes said, but seems to have forgotten that I had said a word –

Mrs. Peyton Randolph seems almost as happy as you are, & hopes you will live in Richmond – But I tell her it would be premature to talk of an establishment for a wife, until you have better secured her. I have not given her or her husband the least suspicion of the actual state of affairs when you last wrote – They say Mr. Tucker can have no objections – to which I reply in some general way so as to give no ground to suspect that I know any thing about his views – I shall expect you on Saturday; but you will do on this head as you please – I will only observe that should Judge Tucker persevere, you had better make an impression as deep as possible on the Mother & daughter, and come up & try the effect of a personal interview with him — I calculate on your invincible & unshaken firmness — Should

you waver, or consent to any modification whatever, I will say truly that I have not heretofore known you — Tell Miss Carter I long for the time when I may call her Sister —
  Yours sincerely
  William H Cabell

Older brother William quite steals the show in the above letter with his great self-assurance and gift for expressing it. But if there is another pleasant image to be taken from it, it may be that of "old Judge" Peter Lyons. Despite having emigrated from Ireland over seventy years earlier, he still retained the Gaelic gift for telling a good story. Cabell, of course, would have focused instead on all the family intelligence and advice. The likelihood is, however, that his reply to St. George, which follows, had been taken to the Williamsburg post office before the above adamant letter from William arrived.

Letter 18: Joseph Cabell in Williamsburg
to St. George Tucker in Richmond

Williamsburg, 7ʰ Nov 1806

My Dear Sir,

I feel infinite regret, on receiving yours of 3ʳᵈ inst., to find that my last has made no impression on your mind, and that we still differ on a subject of so much importance as the conditions on which I am to be united to your amiable Daughter. I am sensible of the impropriety and indelicacy of urging a discussion of such topics, but the respect [I owe?] *to you, to myself, and my friends, imperiously requires of me not to smother the objections I still conscientiously entertain to the proposals you have made me. I would be unworthy of the family of which I wish to become a member were I to be indifferent to the terms on which I am to pass its threshold. And I am sure you will esteem me the more for speaking to on this occasion with the sincerity of a friend, and the independence of a man with the object then of placing my opinion in a stronger light. I respectfully solicit your attention while I review some of its grounds, and reply to the principal observations of your last favor to me.*

The motives of yourself and myself are now out of the question. Feelings are also put out of view, except so far as they are bottomed on substantial reasons. Let the subject rise on us in the light of reason only; and how does it appear?

The great object which Miss Carter and myself propose to ourselves is to live happily together. It must be confessed that anything which in the slightest degree might affect this object ought not to be done without the most evident necessity, and the most invincible reasons for its propriety. Now Sir, let me ask you if a marriage settlement has not this tendency? Is there no inconvenience, no embarrassment, no odium in the existence of separate estates, separate interests, separate accounts between a man and wife? Is it possible for you to censure the man who wishes to avoid such a situation? You do not touch on this subject in your reply to me, yet I consider it all important and sufficient of itself to justify my conduct. I have an elevated idea of the rights and duties of the married state. It implies not only a union of affection, but as complete a union of fortunes as the parties can effect.

You assign as one of your strongest reasons for a settlement that the husband of Miss Carter should not have the power of changing the nature of her property; and this for me is one of the most powerful for opposing the measure. Who could manage the interest of my wife better than myself? Who more tremblingly alive to her welfare than her own husband? Suppose, when married to her, I should be accidentally asked by an old friend, "Where is her fortune?" "Vested in trustees." "Why?" "Because her friends have bestowed her on a man, to whom at the same time they could not entrust the power of altering the description of her property." And who is this man whom they thus bind with odious restrictions?" I would refer for a description of him to your last letter to me.

Your reasons, respected Sir, are very satisfactory as to the imprudence of changing the nature of estates in Virginia. But observe; I do not contend for the power which without a settlement might fall into my hands, because I have any idea at present of calling that power into action; but because it might be prudent to exercise it at a future day; and, in the event of my marriage, I should be the man to whom it ought to belong, in preference to all others on earth. I have never taken an important step in my life without consulting a friend; and is it probable that I should sell the property of a wife, without the best reasons and the best advice? And, Sir, is it rational to suppose that any human foresight could dictate at this moment what ought to be done with an estate many years hence? From the summit of the present, you may see a good way over the dim vale of the future; but it is impossible for you to discern all the incidents which at remote periods might call for changes in our situation in life.

I must continue also to differ with you in opinion as to the effect of the settlement on paternal authority. Here you cite your own experience only; and were the basis wide enough, I would willingly rest the general principal on it. But, my dear Sir, have I right to conclude that I should be as fortunate as yourself? and that in my case a rebellious son could not be urged on to undutiful and ungrateful acts, whenever the idea should flit across his mind, that *he possessed an independence in despite of me? I have ever understood that the power of willing away an estate from children was founded on its necessity to paternal government. I appeal to the general opinion, and general experience.*

The foregoing inconveniencies are inseparable from a settlement, and would press on us at every period of our lives, were we to attain the age of eighty.

In relation to the reasons which induce you to make this demand of me, I agree perfectly with you as to the injustice & inequality of our laws and had I been on the bench with you, during the scenes to which you allude, I would have united in your benevolent feelings and indignant exclamations. But in order to obviate a remote & contingent evil, ought we to expose ourselves to present & certain inconveniencies, when that evil may be avoided in another way, not subject to such inconveniencies? If others have died intestate, must I follow their example? Because others have squandered the fortunes of their wives, shall I of [course] follow in their steps, and be guilty of the same imprudence? As to any debts which I might contract in future, they would be for our mutual pleasure and happiness, and we ought to be mutually bound for them. But, my dear Sir, after what you know of me and what I have said, can you think that these are evils likely to occur? If not, why take precautions that are embarrassing and disagreeable to me; which are desired neither by your daughter, nor by Mrs. Tucker, nor would ever be expected by the connexions of either party? I could never admit that any one would have a right to utter a word on the subject, provided yourself, your Lady, and Daughter are pleased; & these facts ought in my opinion release you from all responsibility in yielding to our united wishes. Instead of those being room for complaint, I trust that my conduct would prove a source of general satisfaction.

I attach the utmost respect to the examples of yourself & Mr. Coalter; tho' you will admit that your own case is not perfectly analogous, as Mrs. Randolph had children by a prior marriage at the time you married her. Your having submitted to the same terms yourself, and your having demanded them of a man of so much respectability as Mr. Coalter, prove that you have ever been uniform in your opinion on this subject, and that you are now governed by pure and honorable motives. But suppose each of you in your respective cases had viewed this matter in the same light as myself; would you not as independent and candid men have acted in the same way? And, Sir, to prove that I am not singular I appeal to the general practice and sentiment of Virginia. It is a fact that settlements are so odious among us that they have been proposed to young men in order to break off matrimonial connexions. I regret sincerely that my conduct on this occasion should surprise you; the more so as it has been approved in the warmest manner by a few persons here for whose head and heart you entertain the highest respect, and who have *come to a knowledge of our difference in opinion in a confidential way. In persevering in the same course I act not from pride or pertinacity but from the honest dictates of my own reason; and I trust that my character, my situation as to fortune, (altho' it is not an opulent one) and my prospects in future life will ever shield me from the imputation of improper motives.*

I ardently hope that my views may now meet your approbation, as they have done that of Mrs. Carter & her Daughter. The first wish of my heart is to take you by the hand & call you by the sacred name of Father. My bosom knows no other than filial sentiments towards you. May they be reciprocated, & discussion be lost in mutual confidence & affection!

I leave Williamsburg tomorrow [Saturday], & in the evening shall be reinstated in my lodging at my Brother's in Richmond. In the interim, I remain, dear Sir, most respectfully and sincerely your friend.

J.C. Cabell

As he said he would, Cabell left Williamsburg for Richmond by stagecoach the next day. He had traveled the same route two weeks earlier in the opposite direction, with no knowledge of whether Polly Carter might become his wife, and that uncertainty remained. He also carried his previous letter [No. 18] with him. There was no better way to be certain of the delivery of that important correspondence to St. George than to see to it himself.

Letter 19: From Joseph Cabell in Richmond
to St. George Tucker in Richmond

Richmond, Sunday Morning [9 Nov 1806]
My dear Sir:

I got up [arrived] *last night some time after dark. I send you a packet from Mrs. Tucker, accompanied by a letter* [No. 18] *from myself, which on perusing she assured me was perfectly satisfactory to her, and which I hope and trust will be equally so to you. I shall be extremely happy to hear from you on this subject as speedily as possible, either by letter, or in a personal interview, as may be most agreeable to you.*

With every assurance of respect & friendship, I remain, Dear Sir,

Very truly yours.
Jos: C: Cabell.

Judge Tucker.
At the Swan

Cabell did not have to wait long for an answer. The Swan, located on Shockoe Hill near the Capitol was one of Richmond's finer taverns, with a history as a favored temporary residence of the judges during court sessions. St. George was a regular guest there, and it would not be a surprise to learn that he used a familiar courier to carry his reply to Cabell.

Letter 20: From St. George Tucker at The Swan
to Joseph Cabell at The Eagle

Dear Sir,

I am this moment favoured with your note accompanied by a Letter from yourself & one from my wife which I have not yet opened. — As soon as I shall have perused them with that attention they deserve, I will either return an Answer, in writing, or solicit the favor of a personal Conversation. Mean time believe me most cordially & sincerely your friend &c. &c.

SG Tucker

Sunday Morning [9 Nov 1806]

We learn here that Cabell was not staying in his room at William's home but at the nearby Eagle Tavern. The late arrival of the stage had likely caused the change of plans. He and St. George were thus just a few blocks apart, and St. George had responded comfortably to Joseph's overture that he would be prepared to meet in person to continue their dialogue.

Letter 21: From St. George Tucker at The Swan
to Joseph Cabell at The Eagle

Richmond, 9 Nov 1806

My dear Sir,

I hasten to reply to your favor of the 7th this moment received, & perused with the attention that it merits. Your arguments, my dear Sir, are not convincing to my Judgment, situated as I am. — Regarding my dear Child in no other light than as my own, I might as a Father possessing an absolute right over her fortune, and believing from the very high opinion I entertain of you, your motives, your Prudence, and your reasons, that I should hazard nothing by the concession, yield my own opinions to your feelings. But considering her, as I must on the present occasion, as the Daughter of another man (from whom her fortune is derived,) whom circumstances have placed under my Care, I can not take upon myself the Responsibility of disposing, unconditionally, of herself and fortune, contrary to the Dictates of my own unbiased Judgment, long since maturely considered, and adopted. I will, however, meet your wishes as far as I possibly can. If then you will promise me on her behalf, in case she should survive you, to have either her present property in Lands & Negroes, or the full value thereof, absolutely, and unconditionally, so that in that Event she may dispose both of herself and her fortune, without restraint, I will so far sacrifice my own Opinions & Judgment to your Wishes, and, I will add, my own. Should you still resist this proposal, I must beg leave to say that those of her friends, to whom her fortune in certain Events will devolve, must be consulted, and their consent & approbation be obtained. If however you accede to my proposal, as I hope and trust you will, no further Bar shall be interposed on my part to your union, & our mutual & general Happiness. I wait your answer — mean time I remain with Sentiments of the most cordial Esteem, and friendship, Dear Sir,

Yours most truly,
S: G: Tucker.

With this note, written within an hour or so of the previous, St. George sought to bring an end to the dispute with Joseph. He offered to accept from him merely a promise, rather than a document, ensuring the protection of Polly's property. St. George's wisdom, patience, and maturity (at twice Joseph's age) were all likely involved in his proposal of this new solution. He was not only an experienced judge, but an experienced father of sons.

Also surely at work would be whatever heartfelt plea Lelia had made (in her cover note that has not survived) for him to find a resolution. It is inconceivable that she would have openly challenged her husband's judgment or marshaled arguments against it. On the other hand, she would have unreservedly expressed the heartache that the disagreement was causing to both Polly and her, thus adding another reason and motivation for St. George to resolve it.

St. George's insistence that, were Cabell not to make the promise, he would require the consent of some of Polly's (blood) relatives before giving his own, was tied to the laws of inheritance. A refusal from Cabell would mean that upon marriage Polly's side of the family would be removed from the chain of inheritance. Were Polly to die *now*, unmarried and childless, her property would be shared with her siblings and parents. Were she (or he) to die without children *after* their marriage, only the members of *his* family would be in line for any distribution of that property. Accordingly, St. George raised the matter of the consent of her relatives. Though he does not say so, he probably would also have required the consent of her guardian, to be appointed by the court in light of the recent death of her uncle and past guardian, Edward Carter. These legalities are explained here because they do come up later.

Letter 22: From Joseph Cabell at The Eagle to St. George Tucker at The Swan

My dear Sir,
    I will send you my reply to your favor of this morning in the course of an hour. In the interim, I am most sincerely yours,
    Joseph C. Cabell

Sunday [9 Nov 1806]
Judge Tucker. Swan Tavern.

And so the Sunday morning exchange continued, with Cabell politely indicating that he had received St. George's note, but needed some time to think before responding to what it proposed. The previous agonizingly slow exchange of letters between two towns had now become a rapid exchange of notes between two taverns. For Cabell the prolonged anxiety caused by waiting for the mail was replaced by the worry of having to write a swift reply to St. George without being able to review it with family or friend.

The Eagle[d] was the best-known tavern in Richmond, built at the same time as Virginia's Capitol in 1786, at the bottom of the hill from it. Its insurance policy issued in 1796 by the Mutual Assurance Society of Virginia, described it as "38 by 62 ft, 3 story high. Walls brick covered with wood."[e] It had a porch running the length of the front, and contained a ball room, a coffee room, and other meeting places on the ground floor. It was also, as we have learned in these letters, the departure and arrival point for the Richmond stagecoaches, and therefore for the mail.

The Eagle was better known for the continuous gambling and drinking that occurred in and around it than for its guest-rooms, which were often occupied by state legislators. A garden, stable, coach house, kitchens and other "office houses" necessary for its operation shared the half-acre on which it stood. Within months of this story, Aaron Burr was held in one of its rooms and examined there by Chief Justice John Marshall in advance of his appearance before a grand jury called to decide whether he should be charged with treason.

The Swan tavern, standing at the top of Shockoe Hill, was less than a ten minute walk across the Capitol grounds from The Eagle at the bottom. Much like the birds after which they were

The Swan Tavern, Richmond. Courtesy of
The Virginia Historical Society[5]

named, The Swan was sedate by comparison with the bird of
prey. It began as a business at about the same time as the Eagle,
but as "a large and commodious house on Shockoe Hill, desig-
nated by the sign of "ST TAMANY." (The Society of St. Taminy
was a social club for patriots formed after the Revolution.) The
Swan also differed from The Eagle in being smaller, at two stories, and built of wood. But like The Eagle, The Swan had the
expected porch that ran the length of its front.

A writer who knew the establishment at the turn of the
century described it as ever neat and clean "and if the table

never groaned under French dishes, nor sparkled with costly champagne, the ham was always prime, meats the very best the market could afford—the cooking unrivalled—and the wine the best London particular imported direct from Madeira..."[6] Over the years, two wings were added to the original rectangular building, as well as two detached dwelling houses. The needed stables and other outbuildings also shared its lot. Based on the character of their lodgings, it seems quite fitting that the older judge and father be housed at the settled and rather private Swan, while the restless young suitor stayed at the lively and quite public Eagle.

Letter 23: From St. George Tucker at the Swan to Joseph Cabell at the Eagle

Sunday Half after One

Dear Sir,

Pardon my solicitude to receive your answer to my Letter of this forenoon, as I fear the mail may be closed, before I could communicate its contents to my Wife & Daughter if not very shortly received.

Your friend most truly,

S: G: Tucker

[9 Nov 1806]

That he wanted time to tell the news to his wife and daughter suggests that St. George was optimistic that Joseph would reply favorably. And Joseph's answer soon arrived.

Letter 24: From Joseph Cabell at The Eagle
to St. George Tucker at The Swan

Richmond, 9th Nov 1806

My dear Sir,

I received your favor of this morning a few hours past; and my sensibility is much excited by the spirit of concili- ation & strain of friendly disposition, which everywhere pervades it.

On my part, I feel every wish which could animate the human heart to meet you on ground mutually satis- factory. The proposition you now make me, however, is only a modification of the one contained in your former letters; and as it was not to the shape, but to the sub- stance of the principle, that I have all along objected, I see no new reasons to dissipate my reluctance. But tho' I hold it improper to bind myself on this occasion by writ- ten or verbal promise, permit me to ask you this solemn question; Do you believe that a man of my character & principles would fail to leave a surviving wife in the most comfortable situation possible? — On this ground I think you may safely stand. — As to the relations of Miss Carter, they ought to feel no other solicitude in this affair, than that she should be well & happily married. Being conscious that the proposition of marriage on my part is humiliating neither to herself, nor her family, and that there is nothing peculiar to this case, which ought to take it off the ground of marriages in general in Virginia, I can have no objections, should you feel disposed, to your consulting her relations on the propriety of such a connexion: & if you think it proper, as a guide for yourself, to obtain their sentiments on the expediency of demanding a settlement in her favor. But tho' I cannot object to your pursuing this course, to relieve your own feelings; I wish it to be distinctly understood that my resolution is taken: for after having refused to accede to such a proposition coming from yourself, I certainly would not submit to it proceeding from any other quarter. I will conclude by observing, that Miss Carter is the only woman on earth to whom I have ever offered myself as a husband; she is the only one I wish to marry; the terms on which I desire to be united to her are honorable in the estimation of our country; my happiness is staked on the event; & it remains with you to decide. I beg you to receive the renewed assurances of my perfect friendship & respect.

Joseph C. Cabell

St. George had to be taken aback by Cabell's negative response to his overture. The father had conceded much to his prospective son-in-law in offering to accept a promise rather than a settlement (legal document), only to have it rejected. Was this really Joseph's position, or had he perhaps not fully appreciated the concession? Joseph was, after all, separated from his usual legal advisors, both his brother William and Wirt. And why was he returning to the theme of expecting the complete trust of St. George? St. George had already assured him that he had it, but that it meant nothing at all to either fate or Virginia law. With all urgency of writing to Lelia and Polly now removed, St. George replied at length to Cabell.

Letter 25: From St. George Tucker at the Swan to Joseph Cabell at the Eagle

Richmond, 9ᵗʰ Nov 1806. Four o' Clock.

My dear Sir,

Your favor in answer to mine of this date is this moment received—I cannot but regret the different views which you & I have taken of the important subject we have discussed. In my letter of this morning my intention was, as I thought, manifest. To guard against accidental Intestacy which might put it out of your power do for a surviving wife what a man of your Character and principles would do, were he to make a will. How many thousands of prudent men, my dear Sir, omit this precaution? — How often does the state of a mans property, in the changes he meditates, amount to an actual revocation of a will, already made? These, my dear Sir, are the Events my sad observation has induced me to wish to guard against. And against them, I can not still but hope you would be willing to guard, by a promise, which will leave you at large to act as you please during your life, and only provides for a Contingency which can not be too early, or too cautiously guarded against. Anxious to place this sub-ject in such a light as to have no room for dissatisfaction on either side, I conjure you to reflect upon it again; think what *might be the Situation of your family if you should happen to die between the period of disposing of property which you will possess, and that of reducing into a perfect Title, or a productive state, that which you might propose to acquire. Remember how intangible Lands are in this Country in Case of intestacy — that should you, with a view to making an Exchange of your property, enter into a considerable contract, your whole personal Estate might in that Case be exhausted, while an <u>unproductive</u> real Estate of ten times the value of the debt may remain untouched. Indeed my friend had you read as many Virginia records, as I have on these Subjects, your apprehensions would take the Alarm from the chance of such Events. With every precaution that prudence can dictate the far greater number of Gentlemen in this Country Seem to me, when they die, to leave their families under some Embarrassment arising from their Circumstances. Indeed, my dear Sir, if you knew my heart, & could participate in its feelings you would find it is not a man of "your Character & principles," but human nature, surrounded by a thousand Casualties & Embarrassments, peculiar to this Country, that I wish to provide against. And I solemnly protest to you as a man of truth and Honour, that could we exchange Situations, I would embrace with Joy a proposal which would enable me, sick or well, embarrassed or unembarrassed, by temporary Circumstances, or disappointments, to fold in my arms the partner of my home, & say, come death, when thou wilt. I have this better part of me provided for. — I have felt that Lamentation my friend,* *too often, not to appreciate it. And I call God to Witness I had rather my dear Wife should enjoy the Independence she will in case of my death, than to own it absolutely, myself. Think me not thus personal, disrespectful, distrustful, or animated by any unkind, unfriendly, or unamicable Sentiment towards you. I long to embrace you as a Son — whose generosity & honor I have the fullest Confidence in — but whom I still know to be mortal. — Promise me that in Case you should die <u>Intestate</u>, she shall be entitled in Case of Surviving you to a <u>certain</u> <u>provision</u>. And if you think the whole of her Lands & negroes more than you would wish absolutely to leave, name the proportion of the latter, or the proportions of both, in case you should sell them. You will still be entitled to a large Sum of money, (perhaps $8 or $10,000) the amount of which I know not, from her Uncle Edward's Estate. Can you hesitate, my dear Sir, to accept such an offer, made from such motives, by a man who in fact possesses no <u>Right</u> to dispose of the Child of his affections, or her property? You do not appear to have given to this part of the subject due Consideration. As a member of <u>my</u> family, I shall receive you with Joy. — but how can I Give you the Daughter of <u>another</u> <u>man</u> without taking upon me the Character and Responsibility of her Guardian? — I must go into a Court & give security in a large penalty, and you would wish me to act against my own Judgment? Surely, my dear Sir, this is requiring more than my good will towards you, as the husband of one most dear to me. Until she arrives at an Age to dispose of herself she must rely on*

some friend to act in that Character. If my Judgment tells me I ought not to dispose of her fortune unconditionally, will you abide by it — consult some other friend — allied to her by blood, but not one who loves her so well; or wait the period when she can dispose of herself and fortune, without imposing upon others this necessity of doing that which their own Experience & Judgment condemns? Indeed, my friend, could we change places, I should instantly throw myself into your arms with thankfulness, and hasten to receive from you, what I deem the highest pledge of Esteem, affection and friendship. That these Sentiments may meet with a reciprocal return in your Bosom, is most truly the wish of your warm & affectionate friend
   S:G: Tucker

would it be agreeable to you to call to see me this Evening? I am quite alone.

St. George here explained in greater detail both the Virginia law and the often adverse consequences for wives should their husbands die without a will (intestate). He wanted Cabell to understand the importance of a legal document that would protect Polly's property, but would consent to her marriage simply upon Cabell's promise to make one. Perhaps he intended to convey the full measure of his trust in Cabell by accepting his word, rather than the deed. He was also beginning to wonder whether Cabell simply did not understand him, as distinct from understanding but disagreeing.

Determined to resolve those questions, if not the disagreement itself, St. George invited Joseph, with unreserved
warmth, to visit him that evening. And Cabell did so. The
next note was penned by him late that night by candlelight,
shortly after returning to his him room at The Eagle following their meeting.

Letter 26: From Joseph C. Cabell at the Eagle
to St. George Tucker at the Swan

9ᵗʰ Nov 1806. Half past nine at night.
My dear Sir;
    My reason having recovered from the tumult of feel-
ing into which I was thrown by our interview, I imme-
diately perceive the reasonableness of the proposition you
have made me this evening. I therefore cordially meet your
wishes; tho' I still believe that the course I would myself
have pursued would have lead to the same point. I will
come over in the morning And I hasten to drop a line to
our beloved friend in Williamsburg. My heart is full of joy.
    most affectionately yours.
    Jos: C: Cabell.

Judge Tucker.
Swan Tavern.

We do not have to imagine the transformation in Cabell's
spirits, for he reveals that himself in his few words. Our only

disappointment is that his letter to "our beloved friend in Williamsburg," meaning Polly, has not survived. St. George was quite surely writing to Lelia when Cabell's note arrived, but he immediately replied to it.

Letter 27: From St. George Tucker at the Swan
to Joseph C. Cabell at the Eagle

I receive with the most sincere delight your note — You know the Consequence. You can ask nothing of me which I shall not bestow with the most Sincere delight & Happiness.
    Most truly & affectionately
    Your friend
    SG Tucker

Sunday night.

Cabell saved the originals or copies of most of the letters in this correspondence, and added notes for his records. From them we learn that St. George had received the previous note from Joseph at 9:30 at night, and that Joseph received his reply at an even later hour. He clearly wanted to preserve his memories of the momentous occasion as it had unfolded, from the time of his anxious arrival in Richmond by stage-coach late the night before to the joy of the present evening. Both men, surely exhausted, went to sleep that night filled with happiness. St. George was the first to put pen to paper the following morning.

Letter 28: From St. George Tucker in Richmond to Joseph C. Cabell in Richmond

Richmond, 10ᵗʰ Nov 1806.

My dear Cabell,

Your little note last night enabled me to sleep Serene, which I have not done before for a fortnight. But, as the object of our long & interesting Correspondence has been not barely to satisfy ourselves, but to provide for Contingencies and Events which neither of us may live to see, it will be proper that in your Reply to my Letters of yesterday, you should be so full, clear, and explicit, that no <u>Interpreter</u> will be necessary, should the occasion happen, to explain our mutual Intentions. — Let me add a Request, that you will subjoin, that in the Events intended to be provided against, my dear Child may enter and take possession of the whole Estate to which She will be entitled, as well Slaves & personal Estate, as real, without the forms & Ceremonies of law, and may hold the same to the sole and proper use of herself and her Heirs, as her own proper Estate, in the same manner as if no marriage ever had, or should have taken place between you.

Your friend &c
SG Tucker

Now comfortable that they had the same objective, St. George entered decisively into the wording of the letter that Cabell would use to describe his intent regarding the treatment of his property should he die without a will. Drawing on his extensive legal experience in both the courtroom and the classroom, St. George proposed content and phrasing to ensure that Polly had sure and immediate control of their property, with no need for a court interpretation. The letter was not addressed as a note being carried between the two taverns. St. George may have been at the Courthouse and Joseph, by now, at his brother's home.

Letter 29: From Joseph C. Cabell in Richmond to St. George Tucker in Richmond

Richmond, 10th Nov 1806

My dear Sir,

Our personal interview of last evening has had the happy effect of reconciling our views, on the interesting subject of our late correspondence. And since My conversation with you, I confess, I more distinctly comprehend the proposition of your favor of yesterday at 4 O'clock. Believe me that I am delighted at the method you have suggested of attaining the great object you have in view, without sacrificing principles to which I am conscientiously attached.

I can assure you that it is my intention as soon as I shall marry your Daughter to make a will, and therein to make such a Provision for her, as her Estate, & my attachment to her will naturally dictate. And in case of change of circumstances, or change of property, it is my intention always to alter my will, so as to ensure her every provision which could be expected from an honorable & affectionate husband. These intentions will certainly ever regulate my conduct. But as I object to the principle of marriage contracts or marriage settlements, I wish it to be distinctly understood that what I have said above, is only a solemn declaration of my intentions: and not a contract or covenant, depriving me of any of the powers, which I would have Possessed, had such declaration not been made.

After your impressive remarks, however, of last evening, tending to shew how many accidents in life may defeat our best intentions, it is my duty and my wish to provide at the present time against the particular contingency to which you call my attention. It is that of my dying Intestate, your Daughter surviving me, and of my being thereby frustrated in my affectionate intentions towards her. I do therefore hereby promise, engage and bind myself and my estate, that if I should happen to die Intestate, she surviving me, this letter shall be a substitute for a will: and that in that case, she shall be absolutely entitled to the whole of her property which I may receive with her in marriage, whether Lands, slaves, or money, as far as the same remain in specie; and as to that part of it which I may use, sell, or dispose of, she shall be absolutely entitled to the full value of it, as the same was sold for; or if money, the same amount, with Interest on the same from the period of my death: and further, that in the event hereby contemplated, she may immediately enter &take possession of the whole Estate to which she will be entitled, as well slaves & personal Estate, as real Estate, without the forms and ceremonies of law; and may thenceforward hold the same to the proper use of herself and her heirs, as her own proper Estate, in the same manner as if no marriage had taken place between us.

I need not describe my happiness at this harmonious close to our correspondence. The scenes which have already passed between us can alone speak for themselves.

I salute you venerable Sir.

Joseph C. Cabell.

Cabell made a full handwritten copy of the important letter before sending it to St. George, adding this comment to the copy he would carefully keep: *Very Important—Being a substitute for a will, provided I should die intestate.* Note that in his opening words, Cabell acknowledged that he had not properly understood the nature and import of what St. George had been insisting upon. Following their personal discussion, he did. And he embraced it, just as St. George had expected of his former student and prospective son-in-law. The impasse that had caused such distress for both them and the women they loved had come to an end.

St. George received the letter, approved of it, and quickly transitioned from relief over the past to joy over the future.

Letter 30: From St. George Tucker in Richmond
to Joseph C. Cabell in Richmond

Richmond, 10ᵗʰ Nov 1806

My dear Sir,

Your favor of this date is now before me: the assurance it contains, united with my exalted opinion of your Character, full Confidence in your honourable attachment and Intentions towards my dear Child, together with a full knowledge of her reciprocal attachment to you, and her wishes upon this subject with those of her mother, will no longer permit me to withhold my Consent to your union. My most cordial approbation, esteem and friendship, you have had from the first. I superadd the last proof it is in my power to give of the same Sentiments, united with a Confidence I could scarcely repose in any other human being. And I hope and trust in God, that a long and happy union between you may prove that I have not done wrong in thus surrendering my own opinions.

Henceforth, my dear Sir, let the enduring name of friend be indissolubly united in our hearts with the affections of a Father & Son towards each other. — Accept the former from me, and believe me ever, yours most truly,

S:G: Tucker

Cabell received this beautiful letter in the evening and most probably shared it with William, Agnes and any of their intimate friends who may have been at the Governor's home. He responded the following morning.

Letter 31: From Joseph C. Cabell in Richmond to St. George Tucker in Richmond

Richmond, 11ᵗʰ Nov 1806

My dear Sir,

On perusing your welcome favor of last evening, I am overwhelmed by sensations of gratitude & delight. Your liberality on this occasion, and the honorable expressions of friendship, respect, & Confidence which you are pleased to use in relation to myself, touch me to the heart, and impose on me the most lasting obligations. It shall be the effort of my life to merit this distinguished proof of your regard: and the approbation of my adopted parents shall constitute the balm of my future days. As to the fair Daughter whom you consign to my arms, I doubt not that we shall glide happily together down the stream of life. My bosom glows with unwonted delight, the idea of thus repairing the ravages of death, in finding a second father in one, towards whom my elevated sentiments of respect & friendship are too well known, to require repetition.

I am most respectfully & affectionately yours.

Joseph Cabell.

This concluded the exchange of letters between St. George and Cabell regarding his engagement to Polly. They were now to be married, and Cabell turned his attention to the obligations placed on him to notify family and friends.

Letter 32: From Joseph Cabell in Richmond
to Bernard Carter at Fauquier Ct. House

Richmond, 12th Nov 1806

My dear Sir;

It has been now many years since I had the pleasure of seeing you, and perhaps you may have lost sight of me. But I must once more present myself to your view, and in a capacity more interesting than that in which I formerly stood. I have lately had the good fortune to become engaged to your amiable Niece Miss Mary W. Carter of Williamsburg, & to have obtained the consent of her Parents, as well as the approbation of my Mother, to our union. The relation which you occupy towards her, & the interest which you feel in her welfare, and which she so highly merits, entitle you to the respect of being informed as to an event on which her future happiness so materially depends. It would give me great pleasure to know, that our contemplated marriage will meet the good wishes of all those whom nature has placed around her as her best guardians & friends.

I am very sincerely & truly yours.
Joseph C. Cabell

Copy of my letter to Bernard Carter. 12 Nov'r 1806.
(N.B. I also wrote to William Carter, brother of Bernard, but
my haste at the moment, prevented me from keeping a copy.)
Bernard Carter esq.
Near Fauquier Ct. House

Bernard and William Carter were sons of Charles Carter of Corotoman and Shirley by his second marriage. They were just two of the fifteen children born to their mother, Anne Moore Carter. Polly's father, George Carter, was one of eight children born to Charles' first wife, Mary Walker Carter. Bernard and William were thus among Polly's many uncles. Having written to them, Cabell now wrote to their mother:

Letter 33: From Joseph Cabell in Richmond to Ann Moore Carter at Shirley Plantation

Richmond, 12th Nov 1806

Respected Mad'm,

You will be surprized to receive a letter from one who is a perfect stranger to you. But my motive in taking the liberty to address you, will, I trust, make my apology. Having the pleasing prospect of being shortly more nearly allied to your family, it would be unbecoming in me, not to give you early information on a subject so interesting to your feelings. I have had the happiness, Madam, to become engaged of late to your truly amiable and much beloved Grand daughter Miss Mary W. Carter of Williamsburg.

Her affectionate parents, Mr. & Mrs. Tucker, and my own worthy Mother, have all been consulted, and been pleased to join in sentiments of approbation respecting our proposed union. The relation in which you stand towards her; your tender affection for her; as well as your anxious solicitude for her welfare, induce me to bow with respect to you on this occasion, & to indulge the fond hope, that you will see nothing disagreeable in the contemplated connexion. I have not the honor of being known to you personally; but it is now many years since I have had the pleasure of being acquainted with your sons, Bernard & William, with the latter of whom I was particularly intimate during his travels in Europe.

I am, dear Madam, with the utmost respect & esteem, your humble servant.

Joseph C. Cabell.

Mrs. Carter's husband (and Polly's grandfather), Charles Carter of Corotoman and Shirley (1732-1806), is not addressed because he had died earlier in the year. His part in the story was nonetheless fundamental, for it is he who, *circa* 1784, gave the Corotoman estate to his son and Polly's father, George Carter. Now, these many years later, his granddaughter's half share in Corotoman would pass to her new husband, Joseph Cabell.

One of the great disappointments in this collection of letters about Polly's betrothal and marriage is that there are no surviving letters from her, and only a few words from her mother,

Lelia, written at the time. With those exceptions, we do not hear the voices or learn the thoughts of the mother or daughter, as they proceeded through these significant and personal events. In Polly's case, this silence is joined by darkness, for there is no surviving image of her made at any time in her life.

The following, written by Polly to her stepfather just a year before her betrothal, is one of her very few preserved letters.

Letter 34: From Mary Walker Carter at Shirley to St. George Tucker in Richmond[g]

Shirley, November 8th 1805

[No Salutation]

I cannot express to you, my beloved Papa, the disappointment I felt when Mr. Hendren told me he had no letter from you. I had fondly hoped to receive one line at least, and I cannot conceal from you that your silence made me quite melancholy. At first I could scarcely refrain from tears, but I comforted myself with the hope that your occupations, and not a forgetfulness of the pleasure your letter would have given me, prevented your sending me such a proof of your affection. — But I will not give way to my feelings, knowing my dear Papa loves me, and I hope tenderly. — I will again be merry, and anticipate the delight I shall feel when Uncle Bernard returns with a long letter from you. — Many many thanks for the shoes and my friends letter. — She only tells me that she writes in Miss Harriet Tabbs sick chamber, and that that young girl is every moment expected to breathe her last.

My poor Uncle has undergone no very visible change since you left us. — His recollection leaves him every morning and he rarely appears to be sensible of any thing passing around him.

I wish I could tell you something entertaining my dear Papa, but I cannot. — I amuse myself with my my [repeated word] *music, books, and pen — and the hours have till today appeared short. Mr. H'n informed me of the arrival of Mr. F. Skipwith in Williamsburg. — His letters to you have excited in me a great wish to see him, and the affection he has professed for yourself and Mama makes me already love him.*

Do, my dear Papa. Let me know if Mary Colston is in Richm'd and mention when you return home. — I begin to feel very impatient to see Mama.

When did you hear from Elm Grove, and how are they all there? I am anxious to know what reception the [babies?] *met with, and how my little Mama is, now that she is oppressed with the cares of so numerous a family.*

I am surrounded by noisy children, which will plead an excuse for blunders, &c, &c. — We all send you much love. Farewel [as written] *my dear Papa. If possible write to me, and say something of Mama from whom I have not heard.*

Your affectionate Child,
M. W. Carter

Mary Walker Carter (Polly) was seventeen years old when she wrote this letter, just a year before she accepted Cabell's proposal of marriage. She mentions many family and friends, including her grandfather Charles Carter and her uncle Bernard, but we shall introduce only two. The "little Mama" was her stepsister, Fannie Coalter, who had just given birth to a second daughter. "F. Skipwith" was her great uncle, Fulwar Skipwith, who had just returned to America following years of service as U.S. Consul to France, having been appointed to that post by Jefferson.

Returning to the present days in which Cabell was fully preoccupied with announcing his engagement, the next voice we hear is that of one of his closest friends.

Letter 35: From Isaac Coles in Washington to Joseph C. Cabell in Richmond

Washington, 10th Nov 1806

Dear Cabell,

I have delayed answering your letter for several days under a continually renewed expectation that each nights mail would bring me a confirmation of the happiness to which you looked forward, or at least some new assurances that the golden dreams in which you have permitted yourself so freely to indulge were not mere "baseless fabricks" — why have you not written me? — is it because some unfortunate incident has thrown a shade over the bright prospect of felicity which was beginning to dawn upon you? — or are you so fascinated with the delightful charm which Love has thrown around you, as to have become insensible to every thing else? — Are those ties which for fifteen years have united us, no longer felt? — Must I now become a stranger to a heart which from our boyish days I have known as intimately as my own? — Surely if you had been sensible of the trembling anxiety I felt you would not have so long delayed to have informed me of a desicion which has been for some time known to you, & which will probably fix the destiny of your life. — Your last letter contains no one fact on which I can fix with confidence, or which will enable me to come to any certain conclusion. The mere predictions of Old women — the dreams of a Lover, nor even the rules of Lavater himself would be taken as evidence in any court of Love. — but yet the confidence which you seem to have acquired (tho' I know not how) is to me a very strong presage of your future success. I know enough of the fair Being to whom you are attached, to be confident that she will never excite expectations which she does not mean to gratify — there is nothing in her nature which can delight in inflicting torture, or in sporting with the best feelings of the human heart. — never have I known greater purity of character — you are indeed most fortunate in having placed your affections on one whom calumny has never dared to assail — of whom no one can speak a syllable of harm — And if (as I hope) you occupy the first place in her Affections, I know no one who can look forward to the future with more confident expectations of felicity — A felicity which I could find it in my heart to envy, if I did not know that my friend was to enjoy it.

Yes, my dear fellow, new ties & new relations will very soon spring up around you. The endearing — the delightful names of Husband — of Father — Being dear to you as your own existence will soon have claims upon you which you will not disappoint, and you will be impelled by every consideration of honor & of duty, to exert all the energies of your mind, & of your character, for their interest & advancement. No longer an insulated Being, standing alone in Society, without responsibility for the applications of your time, you will no longer suffer the idle whim of the moment to lead you from a course of Activity & usefulness. — For myself, I have ever thought such a connexion as you are about to form, afforded the only rational prospect of lasting & continued enjoyment. — From my early youth it has formed the ground work of every little plan of future happiness which I have ever proposed to myself. — you know how long & how ardently I have cherished this idea — but I have been unfortunate — most unfortunate. My dream of love has passed away — but then it has left behind it, suspicion, jealousy, & distrust, that now guard every passage that lead to the heart. I am every day more & more sensible of the change that has taken place in my feelings & character, & more & more convinced that the joys you are soon to taste are probably never to be mine — It was all I asked of fortune — I would have been content to have fixed myself down on my little Patrimony, & to have spent the rest of my life in the calm & tranquil shades of the Green Mountain — Ambitious only of the reputation of a good man & a useful Citizen. — but we are not permitted to be the masters of our destiny, & I know not now what will be my course thro' the world. In viewing the long vista of life, how little how very little is there in the prospect, on which I am disposed to set a great Value.

But I hope you will not suppose that these sentiments have arisen out of any circumstances connected with my present situation — On the contrary — I never was in better humour with myself & the whole world. I have every reason to believe that I stand very high in the Presidents good Opinion & he treats me with the most [torn]*ly. — His conduct is marked by so much delicacy, & his conversation is so frank, so open, so unreserved, that the great Executive Officer is constantly lost in the Man, & I declare to you that some of the most delightful moments of my life have been passed in his company. — But these are transient pleasures, the mere joys of a day; very unlike those which you now so fondly anticipate, which will accompany you in Old age, & even smooth your way to the tomb. — farewell — "May all your ways be the ways of pleasantness, and all your paths be peace."*

    I. A. Coles.

Joseph's close friend Isaac Coles had last heard from Cabell *before* he proposed to Polly. He must be introduced:

Isaac A. Coles (b. 1780) Like Cabell, Coles had been a student at William and Mary, and was from an old established family of Albemarle County. Indeed, his middle initial is said to stand for "Albemarle", and to have been created by Coles to distinguish himself from two relatives with the same first name. Coles and Cabell corresponded often and seriously, with Coles regarding Cabell as a brother. Their friendship went back to their childhood, and they were together in London for a while during Cabell's European tour. Isaac became a member of the bar and practiced law in Albemarle before being asked by his neighbor, President Thomas Jefferson, to serve as his personal secretary. That is the position he held at the time of this story.

Cabell and Coles had shared matters of the heart with each other for years, and this letter gives us a glimpse of their friendship and intimacy. From the surviving correspondence of many figures in this story, one comes away with a definite impression that Cabell turned primarily to his brother on matters financial or political, to Wirt on those of the law, to Cocke on all things agricultural, and to Coles on life and love. These distinctions are not sharp-edged. Cabell's pensive temperament led him to seek the thoughts and reactions of many friends on whatever matter was troubling him at the time. But Coles and Cabell exchanged their deeper concerns with each other in a way that sets them apart. The shared confidences in the above letter are not unusual.

Cabell must have written to Coles before he proposed to Polly, when he was all at sea over whether he "occupied the first place in her Affections," and in fear that she might give herself to another before he ever asked. Coles was thus ignorant of all that had happened since Cabell first set out for Williamsburg. He chastised his friend for leaving him in that worried state for so long, but wanted it understood that he was nonetheless very busy and happy in his position of personal secretary to President Jefferson.

Lavater was first mentioned in a letter by Cabell and now again by Coles. He was neither friend nor relative. Johann Kaspar Lavater was the Swiss author of a popular pictorial text on physiognomy, which proposed that one could know the thoughts of another person from their facial expressions. As a field guide to unspoken feelings, one understands why both Cabell and Coles invoked Lavater's book in their present states of uncertainty.

Letter 36: From John H. Cocke at Swans Point in Surry to Joseph Cabell in Richmond

Swans Point, 17ᵗʰ Nov 1806

Dear Cabell,

Your letter of the 13ᵗʰ I have received and am happy to hear that your correspondence with the Judge has terminated to your own as well as his satisfaction. Taking into consideration the tenacious temper of our much respected friend [Judge Tucker] you may indeed call it a victory to have gain'd your point over him. Ever I am glad I did not know until its happy conclusion that your correspondence continued after what you showed me in Williamsburg, for being apprised of your determination and perfectly aware of the Character with whom you had to deal, I should have foreboded some unhappiness between you.

We will endeavour by all means to be at the party to witness the <u>consummation</u> of your Happiness. Rest assured that the confidential communications of a Friend shall never pass the confines of my own heart.

Your commands to Doctor Barraud &c. shall be attended to. We promise ourselves the pleasure of being with our friends in Norfolk the last of this week or first of next.

I remain your Friend with high regards
John H. Cocke

Once again Cabell had asked that a friend keep to himself something communicated earlier by him. The likelihood is that Cabell had shared with Cocke some of his frustrations with St. George while he was in the midst of their impasse, just as he did in one of his letters to his brother. Now he wished that those thoughts and words be quarantined, if not forgotten, by his correspondents. The downside of being a person disposed to submit private thoughts to the judgment of others is that some disclosures may later be regretted.

Letter 37: From Bernard Moore Carter in Woodstock to Joseph Cabell in Richmond

Woodstock, 23rd Nov 1806

My dear Sir,

I have this day received your favour of the 12th inst. Announcing your engagement & proposed union with my Niece. As she has been ever among my greatest favorites, I must beg leave to assure you that no one can more sincerely participate of that tender Interest, amounting in my breast to somewhat of enthusiasm, with which a generous & annimated affection must ever regard so deserving an object, in a crisis so important and so replete with the promise of felicity.

Her heart is the repository of every virtue, and sure am I, she would never bestow her affections except from the purest motives, and with that noble & implicit confidence which constitutes so estimable a charm in her sex, & which it is our greatest praise to merit with unceasing fidelity.

You surely, Sir, are most content, whom she elects the guardian of her whole happiness, — but her other Friends I have no doubt, will chearfully claim their deserved portion of the most unfeigned Joy & gratulation. — In offering you, therefore, assurances of the highest respect, esteem, & affection, I'm confident I do not more than speak the

general sentiment. But, for myself, I must beg leave to be considered more particularly
    & most sincerely yours.
    B.M. Carter

Mr. Joseph C. Cabell
To the care of
His Excellency
William H. Cabell
Richmond

The tradition that personal letters were not merely communications but compositions held sway among the American gentry at this time. Bernard Moore is perhaps the most formal practitioner of the art form to appear in this correspondence. His use of the word "crisis" is jarring to us, but would not have been to Cabell. While today the term is reserved for negative events, it then was used to refer to any emotionally significant event, good or bad. Bernard considered his niece Polly, one of his "greatest favorites," to be in the midst of a very happy crisis.

Letter 38: From William Brent near Dumfries
to Joseph Cabell in Richmond

Near Dumfries, 24ᵗʰ Nov. [1806]

Dear Cabell,

I have received the promised letter, and wish you every happiness.

Your friend Brent

Given that Brent's own proposal of marriage to Polly ended in disappointment, it is no surprise that he replied with a short note, not a literary work like that of Bernard Moore. But though brief, it is not terse; and it reflects both the friendship and the honor that existed between the two men. Cabell must have promised to let Brent know how he fared in his subsequent proposal to Polly. He kept his promise and Brent, politely and sincerely, congratulated him on the happy outcome.

Letter 39: From Joseph Cabell in Williamsburg to William H. Cabell in Richmond

Williamsburg, 27th Nov'r 1806

Dear Brother,

I am still determined to remain here some short time longer, as there is no particular reason for my coming up immediately, & as I pass my time here in a manner highly agreeable & instructive. Every day convinces me of the propriety of my following Judge Nelson in his excellent course of Lectures during my stay here this winter. It is a pleasant & easy method of reviving my lost knowledge of politics & law; and I do not wish to break off in coming up to Richmond, for a greater interval than is necessary. I am sure you will approve of my efforts, even under my present circumstances, to prepare myself as well as possible for my intended stand [for office] *at Charlottesville. As to the appearance of frequenting a Lecture room, at this late period, I make a mockery of it. I delight to oppose public prejudice in so noble a cause. Mr. Tucker approves perfectly of the plan. Besides, I appear rather in the light of a companion, than as a student, to the Professor. I also appear at the Bishop's lectures on natural philosophy, which I find a perfect feast on every Friday. After some time, I shall endeavor to profit by the society of Girardin, with whom I stand on excellent terms. Such is my plan for the winter & spring. Mr. Tucker goes to Norfolk to-morrow morning. — Tell the Doctor* [William Hare, widowed husband of their sister Elizabeth] *I want very much to see him. We all unite in love to you & my sister.*

> *Your affectionate Brother,*
> *Joseph C. Cabell*

William must have earlier questioned the impression that Joseph would give by sitting in on college lectures at age twenty-seven. But Joseph was at ease and happily ready to continue. Louis Hue Girardin, a French immigrant, taught modern languages, history, and geography at William & Mary at this time. Geography then included geology, a subject of great interest to Joseph, who had explored widely for stones and minerals while in France.

Letter 40: From Joseph Cabell in Williamsburg
to William H. Cabell in Richmond

Williamsburg, [undated] *Nov 1806*

Dear Brother,

I would have sent you a few lines by the last mail, had I not been too much engaged in the society of the old city, to have a leisure moment to spare: and indeed I now write you in great haste for fear of being called to breakfast before my letter will be finished. Mrs. Bird [Byrd] *& myself did not arrive here till after eight in the evening, owing to the loss of one of the Passengers trunks on the way, which caused us to be detained between two and three hours, for the purpose of an ineffectual search. It was probably taken* *off; and mine would have tumbled off in a few minutes if an honest negro working on the side of the road, had not have hailed and warned us of our danger. I am only astonished that these accidents do not happen more frequently: I would engage to rob the stage every morning that it leaves Richmond before the break of day. As I came down I felt why Mr. Wirt had been so impatient as he went up. I bribed the Drivers like himself, and I do not believe that the stage ever came quicker from Smith's to Williamsburg. Mrs. Bird descended at Col. Skipwith's, and I had nothing to do, but send my trunk on to the office, and trip across the way to the Judge's. Here I found my beloved Polly, her Mother, & some company from the neighbouring houses, which discreetly dispersed on my arrival. Mrs. T. sent immediately for my trunk, and I was installed in due form in one of the rooms up stairs. I will say nothing of the scene which took place as soon as I was left alone with my sweetheart. You are too old, & my sister too, to remember these things. Judge Nelson popped in soon after me; and Mr. Tucker by Friday's stage. I was standing talking to Polly, in an animated and amorous style, at the moment he entered, and the first I saw of him was when he clasped her in his arms. Judge Nelson lodges here for the present, and will continue as usual to dine with us. I pass my evenings delightfully in their company, & my mornings in miscellaneous pursuits. I have been at a dance at Judge Tyler's, and have dined with Colo. Carey, who waited on me as soon as I arrived, and at the Bishop's, with whom I am on the best* *footing in the world. He thanks you for your attention to the affair of the state line, & together with Col Carey, Mr. Tyler, &c.. enquires after your health & that of my sister. To day I dine with Mrs. Skipwith. In short I am going on here swimmingly. As to the time of my return, I think I shall defer it till the first week in next month, & probably come up with Mr. Wirt, whom I merely had time to salute in passing; and this will be the more proper, as I shall not return again till near the day of my marriage. To-day I joined Mr. Tucker, & Judge Nelson in a guardian's bond in the court of Hustings, in a penalty of $100,000, with a promise to Mr. Tucker that as soon as I should be married, I would execute a release to Mr. Nelson, who has already to pay more than he is worth on acct. of a similar obligation. In coming out of the Court, Mr. T. and myself walked to & fro, & on the green, discoursing my future plans in life, and especially my place of abode. He wishes me to aim at eminence in the law, assuring me I shall not be rich enough to turn to a mere politician. I told him I meant to begin a Lawyer, & there would be time enough to settle how I should end. As to the place, it is a little singular that we had all fixed in our minds on the same spot. He has all the objections to Richmond, & all the reasons of preference for Charlottesville, of which we had spoken: he does not however dwell much on the political advantage of the situation. But I think he will not oppose my going to the Assembly by the time I could get there. He wishes me after some years to move to the Capital, &*

enter the superior courts; but of this, Governor, you know I have not the least idea. However, all this is entre nous. His conduct to me is truly like that of Father, & I will do all in my power to please him. Polly knows of the plan, & like a good wife has given her consent. Show this to my sister in a corner. It is understood that I am to spend the winter here, and that we all move up the country together next summer, visiting you <u>en chamin</u>. I suppose there is not a doubt of my making Charlottesville & its vicinity the chief scene of my future days. Girardin means certainly to leave the College, & has commissioned me to take a view of Richmond, on coming up, as a suitable place for him to establish an Academy. I have proposed to him the upper country, & he does not object, provided he may succeed in buying a little plantation, and rearing his seminary. Shall we place him in the Academy at New Glasgow, or connect him with Ogilvie, & establish them at Charlottesville? I wish to do the latter. Think of this. Now that I am determined to settle up the country, you go of course; so tell my sister to make up her mind, to go too. "I had rather," said Caesar, "be the first man in a village, than the second in Rome." This is surely applicable to our subject. Mr. Tucker sends his best respects to you both, & says he counts on your coming down. Mrs. T. & Polly send their love. My best wishes attend you both; & Upshaw, & Mr. Wirt, & Col. Gamble's family, & all friends.

Yours affectionately,
Joseph C. Cabell

There is much in this letter that will remain without elaboration, the nature of a Guardian's bond, the interest of Girardin in starting a school, and Cabell's belief that he and Polly would ultimately settle in the upper country, coupled with his encouragement to his brother to do the same after completing his term as Governor. The Corotoman estate, on the other hand, is not mentioned but deserves a comment. Though Cabell was apparently of a mind not to settle upon it, its worth could serve as security for other transactions. It would enable him, for example, to take upon himself Judge Nelson's obligation in the mentioned guardian's bond, or to purchase a home. In his usual way, Cabell was pondering over matters of consequence, and testing his ideas—here with William and Alice, while enjoining them to keep his confidences to themselves. Colonel Gamble was Robert Gamble, father of both Alice and Elizabeth (Wirt's wife), and of sons who were also part of the Richmond circle.

Letter 41: From Fanny Bland Coalter at Elm Grove to Joseph Cabell in Richmond

Elm Grove, 24ᵗʰ Nov 1806

Your very flattering letter my dear Mr. Cabell reached me, together with a large packet from Mama, on the same subject. I had been prepared for the information they contained, and with anxious expectation broke their seals. Your attention is unexpected, but it has served to complete my gratification on the present occasion. — Suffer me to offer my most heart-felt congratulations on your approaching happiness, and earnest wishes for a continuance of it; in witnessing my beloved sister's union with you, I shall look forward with certainty to her enjoyment of as perfect felicity, as this world is capable of affording. — Her welfare has ever been a subject of anxious solicitude to me, as nature could scarcely have added strength to my affection for her.

Mr. Coalter participates in every friendly sentiment, and bids me say nothing at present foreseen, shall prevent our being with you on the 1ˢᵗ of January. — We will set out as soon as possible after his return from Botetourt, where he must be on the 15ᵗʰ of Dec'r: I therefore cannot hope to reach Williamsburg sooner than the 24ᵗʰ, when with pleasure I shall hope to renew our former acquaintance — having always recollected you with partial regard — Perhaps you are not aware that in meeting me as your Sister, you will subject yourself to having the venerable title

of Uncle bestowed upon you, by my two daughters, both of whom have taken lessons already, on the score of duty and affection for you — I know not what I have written — My heart is so full, as alike to bewilder my head and unsteady my hand, which I am sure has but illy portrayed the feeling, with which I am most truly your friend
    Fanny Bland Coalter

Cabell's letter *to* Fanny has not survived, but more regrettable is that the packet of correspondence sent to her by her stepmother Lelia is also not to be found. As noted earlier, we learn no thoughts of the bride and very few of her mother in the course of this story. The missing packet surely contained both.

The most extensive letter written by Cabell at this time was sent to his friend and soon to be relative (as Lelia's cousin), Fulwar Skipwith. Skipwith was then the U.S. Consul to France, living in Paris, where the two men had formed a close friendship during Cabell's European sojourn.

Letter 42: From Joseph Cabell in Williamsburg to Fulwar Skipwith in Paris[h]

Williamsburg, 1ˢᵗ Dec 1806

My Dear Sir,

Tho' you were nearer the coast of France, than I to that of America, when we were both on the seas, it does not follow that the obligation of writing was entirely on my side of the water. It is true that you were the oldest of the two; but this must have given you the advantage in facility of writing. You were also married: but this is an advantage you will not boast of for very long. In short, I am writing to compound the matter with you, on any terms that may not vitally affect the honor of either party, on the express condition, however, that our correspondence shall go on in future.

If a letter which I wrote to you from New York has not miscarried, you will have heard of my safe arrival at that place about the 20ᵗʰ May, after a short & agreeable passage of 31 days. I was mortified to find on landing that you had not long before sailed in the Hornet for France. All the dispatches which I had for your from Mrs. Skipwith and others, I brought along & confided to the care and discretion of Gen'l Mason of Georgetown. In passing thro' the seaports I heard frequently of you from persons to whom you had become personally known, and I found that you had every where made a very favorable impression. I spent a few days in Washington, and received very pointed attentions from Mr. J. [President Jefferson] *and Mr. M.* [Secretary of State, James Monroe] *with whom I endeavoured to strengthen their good opinion of my distant friends, and to blast their enemies in France. One happy day was passed in the company of our valuable friend Col. Mercer in Fredericksburg, who retains a very strong recollection & fondness for his friends in Paris. His intention of opposing Dawson, must have been announced to you before you sailed; it is said to be doubtful whether he will succeed. I found my much beloved and respected brother in Richmond, by whom I was received with every possible demonstration of joy and affection. I was much pleased to find an amiable and valuable woman in his second wife. My arrival in Richmond was honored by many marks of attention from most of the eminent men whose scattered residences mark the romantic hills. I there found our friend Upshaw, rising above the unjust imputations against him in his affair with Jones, and steering a more prudent, steady, and successful course, than I had anticipated from his strong mind, agitated by his tempestuous passions. It has been of much service to him, by making him bow with more respect to the opinions of the world. I think he will now make a valuable man, and have his success much at heart. He still talks of moving towards New Orleans, but it is probable that his superior respect for the society of Virginia, will long retain him in this part of the Union. From him I learned that Smith had lately established himself in Urbanna; that Thruston had settled*

in Winchester, where his commencement was not equal
to the expectations of his friends; and that Berkeley, after
trying the practice of physic in Baltimore, had married a
young lady in that place, and moved with her to her estate
in Frederic County in Virginia.

After a short stay with my Brother, I went in the month
of June to the upper country, with the double view of seeing my worthy Mother & other relations, and of passing
away the summer in that healthy climate. This I did with
great satisfaction. My friends have every where given me
so cordial a reception, that I love old Virginia, even more
than ever. I found the mountains of our native state nearly
as agreeable a summer residence as the interior of France.
I made a visit to Monticello, and also to Bizarre. As soon
as the season would admit, I returned to the lower country,
and it was after my arriving a second time in Richmond,
that I encountered the cause that has attracted me once
more to this old and agreeable city. Would you believe that
I am already under an engagement of matrimony to the
daughter of your much admired relation Mrs. Tucker, of
whom we used to speak so frequently & so highly in your
house at Marly? It is a fact that Miss Polly Carter & myself
are to be united in marriage on the first of next month.
You did not see her while here, but must have had some
account of her from your friends; which you will oblige me
by communicating to Mrs. Skipwith; for she was so kind
as to make some enquiries as to my matrimonial views,
in the last note I received from her in Paris, & which I

never had an opportunity of answering. We shall remain here for some months, and probably settle in the course of the next autumn, in the country of the South West mountains, where I mean to set out in the practice of law, but shall probably not remain many years a member of the Bar. God grant, that in the various vicissitudes of human affairs, it may be our fortunate lot to have you and Mrs. Skipwith as our next door neighbours! I am weary of the world, and wish to retire with my beloved wife, and a few friends around me, to some sequestered situation, where I may reconcile with the active duties of a citizen, those sedentary habits, on which my chief views in life ultimately repose.

Your friends here are generally well, except Col. Skipwith, who is troubled with an habitual Diarrhea. I am once more on the most friendly terms with his family. Your relation Peyton Skipwith lately passed thro' Richmond, with his amiable wife, on a trip to Boston.

What has become of your claim? How do you & Gen'l Armstrong stand? I fear from late letters from Charles Carter to his friends that your prospect is a bad one. Are you coming to live among us? How comes our friend Mr. Barnett? And Mr. Warden, & Mr. Sullivan, & Mr. Bowdoin's family? Where is our friend Maclure, whom I value so highly, and think of so often? I wrote him a long letter from the mountains, and will send him another before many weeks are over, by the way of Washington. My other friends must for the present be satisfied to hear

of me thro' the medium of my letters to him, to you, & my
intended brother Charles Carter: but let me assure you
all that my heart glows with intensity for you, and that
you have no better friend than myself. Tell Mr. Maclure
that in becoming a Lawyer, I shall not lose my love for the
sciences, and that if he will send me the promised box of
minerals, I will make the best use of it for my individual
instruction, & the public advantage. My best wishes ever
attend you & Mrs. Skipwith, & your venerable parents;
and I add to them those of all Mr. Tucker's family. Should
you have an opportunity, I will thank you to tell Mr. &
Mrs. Sauvage, that I have been so long out of this country,
that the nightingales are all afraid of me; however I hope
to get hold of a couple of them before long, & will send
them to Brussels.

J'envoie des baisers a Mad'lle Lelia, et a la jolie petite,
et je vous embrasse [I send kisses to Mademoiselle Lelia
and to her little sister, and I embrace you my dear
friend.]

Mon cher ami,
Joseph C. Cabell

Though sent on 1 December 1806, this letter was not received
by Skipwith until June 1807. The other mentioned letters
that also crossed the ocean, from Cabell to his future brother-
in-law Charles Carter and from Charles to his friends, have
not survived, making this one especially valuable. It not only
reveals just how deeply transatlantic correspondents were

dependent on both sailing ships and each other for communication, but also provides unique details on Cabell's speedy transition from being an avowed bachelor to an engaged man. And contrary to the uncertainty conveyed in other correspondence, Cabell presents himself to Skipwith as quite settled on the questions of both his future career and where he would make his home.

We also learn more about Dr. Upshaw, remain in the dark about "the unjust imputations against him," and need learn nothing more about the large catalogue of friends and acquaintances in both Virginia and France who are mentioned. Fulwar Skipwith, on the other hand, would have felt an explicit obligation to convey Cabell's news to his friends abroad, if not provide direct answers to Cabell's enquiries about them. That was expected of friends separated by oceans.

The next letter, by contrast, was close to home—and from a person much closer to Cabell than Jefferson or Monroe.

Letter 43: From Hannah Cabell at Midway
to Joseph Cabell in Richmond

Midway, 9ᵗʰ Dec 1806

Dear Joe,

I received a letter from you some time ago which I should have answered last mail but was too much engaged Changing my abode. I am now fixed here but your brother George has not yet arrived. My carriage is gone for them but the weather is so cold that I fear it will be some days before they come. I have mislaid your letter but I think you gave me a small Invite to see you married but it is out of the question at least this season of the year. I wish you all the happiness the married state can afford and hope to see her when convenient to you and herself, but why will you continue to forget your Old friends, not a word yet of Mrs. Tazewell, pray do no forget her the next time you write. All friends in these parts are well, I have wrote my self almost blind, this is the fourth letter I have wrote to night give my love to your Dulcinea, my best wishes attend you from your affectionate Mother

H. Cabell

The Cabell family did place Polly in high literary company. In Joseph's opening letter he likened her to Helen of Troy from Virgil's *Aeneid,* ("The image of the girl I love, was constantly flitting around my bed. *Three times did I attempt to embrace it; three times did it vanish in air*"), and here Hannah alludes to her as Dulcinea from Cervantes's *Don Quixote*. On the other hand, she knew her son too well to treat him as an angel. He received yet another scolding for including no news of her Williamsburg friends in his letters.

Letter 44: From St. George Tucker in Williamsburg to Joseph Cabell in Richmond[i]

Williamsburg, 15th Dec 1806

My dear Cabell,

I thank you cordially for your little note, & when you have leisure & matter for a longer letter I shall thank you for such a one. We are all very well — and all very busy — I'm having one end of my house pulled down; I hope it will stop there. But at present I may be said to be completely in her [illegible: *hands?*].

Best regards, & kind salutations to you, & your friends from our little Circle.

Very truly & affectionately Your friend &c

S: G: Tucker

P.S. Henry writes — "that he hopes to be here in person to give Evidence of the happiness he feels at the union of his friend & his Sister — and excuses his congratulations till he sees us all."

Beverley writes — "that he has never had Leisure to write since the receipt of your letter till the 6th Inst. He begs I will apologize to you <u>when</u> I <u>see you</u>, for his apparent neglect in not writing, which he should have done long ago, notwithstanding his want of time, had he known *where to direct. That he must therefore defer his thanks for your letter till he shall give you the fraternal embrace." Nelson just returned well, & sends his regards.*

Correspondents often felt obliged to apologize if they wrote only a brief reply to a letter, especially if the subject matter deserved more attention. Thus Hannah offered an excuse for her brevity in declining her son's invitation to the wedding; and St. George forwarded the excuses of his sons for the brevity and tardiness of their replies to Cabell's news.

Cabell did not wait for Isaac Coles to offer his excuses for not writing. He chided his close friend in advance.

Letter 45: From Joseph Cabell in Richmond to Isaac Coles in Washington

Richmond, 20ᵗʰ Dec 1806

My dear Coles;

The Box which will bring you this contains three small collections, taken from my Swiss Herbarium, for Mr. Thomas, M. Randolph, Doctor Mitchell, and Doctor Barton. I beg you to take out the two parcels, destined for the two former, which lie on the top, and are marked with their names, and charge yourself with the delivery of them and then filling up the box with waste paper, to commit it to the care of some gentleman going on to Philadelphia, to be by him delivered to Doctor Barton. You have acted but little like a friend of late in not answering my letter; and in not even saying in reply to my invitation whether you

could come to my wedding. I leave this [place] *in a week for the old city. Farewell you miserable old Batchelor.*
Your happy friend,
Joseph C. Cabell

Isaac A. Coles esq.
Secretary to the President
Washington

In the course of a few sentences we get a show of Cabell's characteristic conscientiousness and orderliness, to which happiness had now been added. The boxes probably contained seeds from European plants, which had been requested by friends, and which he carried back to Virginia from his travels. The following letter from Coles to Cabell crossed his in the mail.

Letter 46: From Isaac Coles in Washington to Joseph Cabell in Richmond

Congress Hall, 24ᵗʰ Dec 1806

Dear Cabell,

Colo. Goodwyn has just informed me that he will leave this [place] to day for Petersburg. He has consented to take charge of the little presents which Mrs. Skipwith sent by you from France, & which you requested me to get of Gen'l. Mason. Colo. Goodwyn has promised to leave them with your Brother, in Richmond, & I hope they may reach you in time to be presented as a new year's gift to the persons for whom they are intended.

The busy scene in which I am engaged here puts it out of my power to accept of your invitation or even to be absent for a day. I wish most ardently to see and to converse with you, but I cannot even look forward to the time when we shall meet; I fear however it cannot be sooner than the last of summer or the beginning of the fall — I have only time to add a thousand good wishes for your happiness, & for the happiness of the fair Being who is destined to accompany you in your journey thro' life.

Your friend
I.A. Coles

St. George also wrote a short note to Cabell in Richmond on Christmas Eve, asking him to deliver two enclosed letters to others. In a postscript, written in French, he asked with some urgency: "By the way! Have you thought about the wedding ring? In chatting with [blank: *Polly*] she denies that you spoke about it with her." We never get an answer, but should trust that the matter received ample attention in Cabell's ever detailed mind. On Christmas Day in Paris, Charles wrote home, utterly unaware of what was happening there.

Letter 47: From Charles Carter in Paris to Lelia Tucker in Williamsburg[j]

Paris, 25th Dec 1806

My dearest Mother,

I should feel satisfied could I hear that you and all my other dear friends were as well as I am myself. — Since I wrote to you I have been very deeply engaged in my studies. In addition to my former occupations I manipulate three hours a day in the laboratory of Mr. Vanquelin, whom you doubtless know by reputation. I thought this would be most useful to me in my Profession. To-morrow I commence dissection between which and Chemistry I shall divide the time which I find I have as equally as possible. These are the sciences for which the French are more renowned than for any others, and perhaps than any other people. — Nothing will be necessary but attention on my part to enable me to leave Paris next November when I shall probably go to Edinburg to complete my studies. — I have just returned from Mr. S.'s [Fulwar Skipwith?] where I went to enquire if there was any opportunity by which I could send the things which you wrote for. Mr. S.

thinks that I will not have one before February when if one offers which I think safe I will certainly send them. You have I dare say been expecting my likeness for a long time. I have not yet had it taken because indeed in these critical times I could not afford to have it done. I went a few days ago to my Bankers to see whether I could draw any money and was again told that it could not be done till some change took place in the Decree which I informed you in my letter by Mr. Browne had been issued by the Emperor [Napoleon Bonaparte]. *The House lent me a few pounds however on my signing the Bills which they had in their hands belonging to me. I gave them a receipt for money they lent me as being a payment in part of the sum contained in my letter of credit. I shall go to-morrow to judge of the terms on which my Bill can be negotiated, and if I find them advantageous, shall accept them. The amusements of the season are not very numerous. There is a Play every night, and once a week a mascarade which, as it is a novel thing, I sometimes go to. Tho' I never take an active part in them, I feel a good deal amused, for the national character is admirably pourtrayed by this institution. — Having dwelt long enough on other sub-jects, I will now ask you a few questions relative to home folks. Brother B* [Beverley], *is he married and is his wife a fine woman? Pray let me have information on both these points. My Sister, has she had any more Admirers, and has she yet found one with whom she is pleased? If she has not, I am afraid she has let all the good opportunities escape. My advice to her is to not marry any one who has*

*been long in Europe, and particularly in France. Tell her
that I have the most utter aversion to her uniting herself to
what we call, in America, an accomplished Man. — You
are all too silent about family affairs. By the bye, my dear
Mother, in August next I shall be entitled to have the tract
which you all ways told me, I should have at that age. As
you reserved it for the years of maturity, I can't help attaching great importance to it. — Do send me in your next a
lock of your's, my Father's, and two Sister's hair of which I
wish to have something made . . .*

    believe me, ever with affection your Son,
    C. Carter

The letter conveys the uncertainties of being an American in
Paris during the Napoleonic War years. Embargoes, blockades,
tariffs, and more conspired to make both communication and
financial transactions difficult. That Charles was in Paris, and
not Edinburgh where he began, was a change he made on his
own, for health reasons. Like his stepbrother Beverley, and
unlike Henry, Charles did not subscribe from an early age to
his stepfather's model of manhood as self-disciplined, reserved,
rational, and industrious. At this time, enjoying life remained
more in his nature. He probably felt the need to tell his mother
that he was applying himself to his studies, knowing that she
would suspect the opposite.

    His admonition to his sister at the end of the letter reflected
his free spirit. The description of the kind of man he wanted
Polly to absolutely avoid as a spouse, not only differed from
himself, but applied so well to Joseph Cabell that we might

wonder whether it was aimed at him. Cabell met with Charles in Paris shortly before returning to America. Did he then stir up Charles' disapproval for being an "accomplished Man?"

Letter 48: From Joseph Cabell in Richmond to St. George Tucker in Williamsburg[k]

Williamsburg, 28th Dec 1806

My dear Sir;

The morning after I last wrote you I repaired to the house of Doctor Brockenbrough and Col. Hilton, before the hour of nine, & delivered your letters agreeably to your desire. Since that, I have met with the Doctor, who has informed me that he will send you an answer, when I come down again.

As I shall so soon be with you again it would be almost superfluous for me to write you at this time were it not to mention a subject in which my feelings are somewhat interested, & which perhaps I would have done better to touch on, at an earlier period. On Thursday next the marriage ceremony between your Daughter & myself will take place; and unless yourself or Mrs. Tucker should feel an objection, or unless there should be a manifest impropriety in the measure, I should feel a particular gratification, which I believe would be common to Miss Polly, in calling on our mutual & valuable friend Mr. Madison to perform the ecclesiastical duties on the occasion. He is one of my oldest & best friends, from whom I have received manifold & inestimable services, & for whom I entertain the most sincere & respectful regard. I should be always happy to

give to such a man a proof of my feelings towards him; &
should this opportunity of showing him my preference be
lost, another may not speedily occur. I know Mr. Bracken
is the Parson of the Parish, and it might appear irregular
and disrespectful to pass him over: but as I never received a
single mark of attention or friendship, which would place
me under the smallest obligation to him, I do not hold
myself bound to violate my own wishes in order to preserve
an unnecessary etiquette towards him. You are in habits
of friendship with both the gentlemen; & if you should
feel any delicacy on this subject, I should be willing for it
to be mentioned that the Bishop would be engaged by my
particular desire. On that day, I wish my nearest friends to
stand nearest to me. Should yourself or Mrs. Tucker have
no repugnance to this proposal, I will thank you sincerely
to give Mr. Madison an intimation, that we shall expect
him to do us the honor of uniting us on Thursday next.

I did not attend to the business of procuring a license
before I left Williamsburg. But it may be done early on
Thursday morning.

I hope my friends in Williamsburg will not be sur-
prised if few or none of my immediate connexions will
attend my marriage. Except my brother [William] *&*
Uncle [Edward] *of this place, they all reside at distance*
in upper country, and could not be induced by any thing
less than an invasion to turn out & travel so far at this
season of the year. My Uncle of this city may be com-
pared to an immense East Indiaman, under heavy sail,
ploughing the waves with inexpressible difficulty. He is

no light active frigate that bounds swiftly over the rolling billows. As I am one of his favorites, as well as Miss Polly, & he was much pleased at the idea of our proposed union, the happy idea once crossed his mind of yielding to our friendly summons. But a thousand difficulties have since sprung up, which I believe would in his mind be sufficient to prevent his attending any wedding at sixty miles distance on earth. My Brother will certainly accompany me, & nothing will prevent him, unless a certain project should be attempted in the interval, of which I will speak to you confidentially when we next see each other. Such are his pressing engagements here, that it will be impossible for him to stay more than a couple of days. Several of my young friends will come down. My Brother [torn: William] will reach Williamsburg on Wednesday evening. I should a[torn: arrive] sooner, but I have promised to perform my quarantine here to the last possible hour.

The most heartfelt good wishes of myself & of all this family attend you & the happy circle now assembled around you.

With the most sincere respect & friendship I remain,
Joseph C. Cabell

P.S. Werg, the Taylor, has just handed me a bundle to bring you.
Judge Tucker
Williamsburg
Care of Mr. Furlong as far as New Kent Ct. House

St. George Tucker docketed this letter with the note "Complied with." Cabell's relaxed, if not last-minute, arrangements for the wedding ceremony are probably a true reflection of where that detail stood in his mind's order of importance. Weddings of the Episcopal Church at this time were normally held in homes, so Bishop Madison would not have been surprised by the venue; and, knowing Cabell as he did, may well have anticipated both the request and its rather late arrival.

That Lelia and Polly had much more to do than Cabell in order to prepare for the occasion is a certainty. The event is best imagined as a church ceremony held in a home followed by a ball with much dancing, eating and drinking. It would have carried on well into the night, if not into the following morning, with many of the family guests sharing rooms, and even the few beds, with other relatives. Some of the relatives and the newly married couple then remained as guests in the home for days, if not weeks, afterwards. But in advance of the occasion, the tradition that the groom not see the bride on the days just preceding their union was already established. Cabell was "in quarantine."

The Richmond uncle, who Cabell so entertainingly described, was Col. Edward Carrington, on his mother's side of the family. As a Revolutionary war veteran, his travels in that cause provided more than enough of an excuse for him not to travel to a winter wedding as he neared the age of sixty. His involvement in the public affairs of the new nation were extensive and continued beyond both the war and the marriage of his nephew. Washington, Jefferson, and Madison were among Uncle Edward's familiar correspondents.

Cabell's mother had already declined the invitation for the same reason as her brother Edward, but she wrote again to her son on the eve of the wedding.

Letter 49: From Hannah Cabell in Warminster to Joseph Cabell in Williamsburg

Midway, 29ᵗʰ Dec 1806

Dear Joe,

Before you receive this you will be no more a batch-elor. — and what shall I say on the subject [than] to say I wish you joy, these words has been handed down from genneration to genneration untill quite worn out and far too cold to convey my feelings. I will therefore say nothing of the kind, you know me and can judge of my wishes for your happiness. tell my new Daughter Polly Cabell I love her already and long to see her and sorry that the distance is so great that I cannot see her until the Spring. I do not know where you intend to settle, but settle where you will you shall sometimes have my company.

I receiv'd a letter from you by last post wherein you lay great stress on the word Small you must have mistaken my meaning, you have a small Invitation it is true but a Sincere one, more was not requir'd for too reasons, you knew I did not require more, and you knew I could not go at this time, and let us drop the subject and ask you the third time, Why, why, why will you forget your Old friends the last accounts I had of Mrs. Tazewell were from yourself

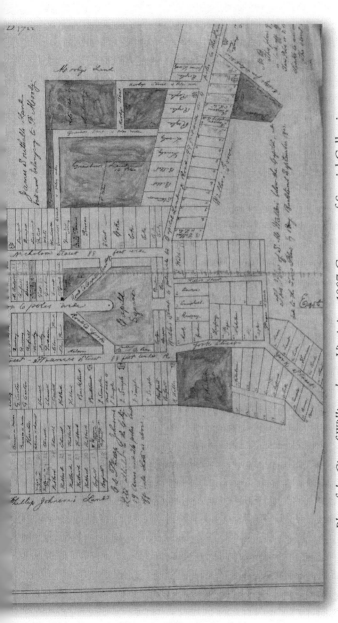

Plot of the City of Williamsburg, Virginia, c1807. Courtesy of Special Collections, John D. Rockefeller Jr. Library, The Colonial Williamsburg Foundation.[6]

some months ago and very unfavourable, when your fate is intirely fixt I hope you will give me some account of her. All your friends in these parts joins me in love and good wishes from your aff't [affectionate] *mother*
   H. Cabell

The wedding took place as planned on 1 January 1807 at the Tucker house, with Bishop James Madison presiding. The ever-welcoming home was filled to the corners with family and friends, even though the Cabell relatives were few. Polly's stepbrothers Henry St. George Tucker and Beverley Tucker were there. Her stepsister Fannie Coalter with her husband John planned to attend, but were frustrated by the winter weather in the west country. We learn that the same proved true for some others, traveling from the east.

Letter 50: From Philip Barraud in Norfolk
to St. George Tucker in Williamsburg

Norfolk, 3 Jan 1807

My Dear Tucker

No apology can be necessary for my not gracing the Nuptials of sweet Poll & her worthy Cabell when Maria Byrd & Nancy & John have not been able to get to you in despite of sundry attempts, by land & by water. The disappointment has been keen and severe. At one moment they had reached you within a third of the way when the fierce elements bore them back to me like a bad penny. They however have malevolent designs on your [torn: *puddings?*] *& plumb cake & if I mistake not you will have enough of them before the affair is over. As I could not get a bit of the first cut excuse me from sharing the scraps and the leavings. Notwithstanding I wish you all to be as happy as I have been for a month & more & as I mean to be whenever I have a chance. You will not be better off. God bless you all. Tell Cabell to kiss his wife for me & you may do the same for me with yours for which she will thank.*

Aff't [Affectionately] *yours*
P Barraud

Nancy was the daughter of Dr. Philip Barraud and John was her husband, John Hartwell Cocke. We thus learn not only that St. George was deprived of the company of one of his closest friends, but so also was Cabell of one of his. Another Cabell guest, who was most definitely expected to attend, also did not do so. He was promptly chastised by Joseph in letters that have not survived. We are, however, able to enjoy his response to the scoldings.

Letter 51: From William Cabell in Richmond to Joseph Cabell in Williamsburg

Richmond, 18th Jan 1807

My dear brother,

I received your second letter last night, and think with you that we have acted most shamefully in not writing to you, but as I do not like the business of abusing myself, I will impose the task on you, hereby agreeing to plead guilty to every charge. I must say however that I have been incessantly engaged, & that altho I have not before written there was never a day in which I did not <u>intend</u>, and that is as far as I go in a great many other matters. So you must take the will for the deed. But do not think because we have been silent that we have been unmindful of you and the scenes in which you were engaged. We have wished you joy a thousand times & participated in it as often. We have never taken a glass of St. George in our family circle (and when was the day that we did not) but "Jo and his Polly" have been toasted with full hearts & flowing glasses. I lament that it was not in my power to witness your happiness. God bless you both and make you as happy as you deserve. Give Polly a sweet kiss and *an affectionate embrace for me, & convince her that I love her as my sister. By the bye, what would you say if I should step down to Williamsburg some time in next month, before I go to Amherst? But do not calculate on it, for my motions are extremely uncertain. I assure you however that such a trip would give me infinite pleasure, and if it shall be out of my power to go down, you must come up here about the 4th day of March, not withstanding all the jibes & jeers to which you might be exposed. The Doctor will leave us some time next week and so will Miss Kinney. They all wish you every happiness. Agnes sends her love to you & your Polly and wishes to know whether you have commenced your system of government. She has many complaints against you for the pernicious doctrines you advocated in my presence, and is determined if possible to defeat you in your plans with respect to your own wife, if she can have any influence over her.*

When the Assembly rises I will give you some tiresome letters. I am at present very much engaged. Our best respects to Mr. & Mrs. Tucker, Mr. & Mrs. Coalter, Judge Nelson &c.

Yours sincerely
W H Cabell

P.S. Hector Cabell is dead – a circumstance not to be regretted considering his habits

What information might add to the enjoyment of this letter? A glass of "St. George" was wine, probably Madeira, which Joseph had recently procured in quantity for his brother. The nickname for it may have been particular to St. George Tucker's circle of friends. For he was known to both enjoy it and to give it as a gift, having imported it from his homeland of Bermuda. His father had established a vineyard on the island to produce it locally.

And what of Joseph's "pernicious doctrines" on marriage? It is a good guess that he held the longstanding view that husbands stood in loving but paternalistic authority over their wives, and had declared his position to Alice. Alice was a Gamble by birth and thereby not at all likely to have agreed with him. Recall that her sister was married to William Wirt. Historians have written at length on the correspondence between those two, which firmly places them in the vanguard of taking marriage to be a partnership between equals. Alice plainly stood with her sister on that matter.

Hector Cabell (b. 1768) was a cousin who had earned a reputation in the family for his irresponsible ways. His troubles were related to drinking, and that may have led to his death reported in the above letter. The visiting Miss Kinney was probably Matilda Kinney (b. 1789), daughter in a prominent family from Albemarle County whose members were longstanding friends and neighbors of the Cabells.

Not long after the wedding, St. George replied to a letter sent by daughter Fannie [Coalter], with a view to Lelia adding a postscript. He told Fannie that all remained in high spirits, amplified by the arrival of their Jamestown friends, the Amblers, who had recently moved to Richmond; but diminished by the fact that "your Mama caught a violent cold on Tuesday by having every door & window in the house open to one of the dampest warm atmospheres that ever came at this season." Lelia had her own thoughts on the matter.

Letter 52: From Lelia Tucker in Williamsburg to Frances Bland Coalter in Staunton[1]

15th Jan 1807

P.S. All are gone to the Bishops [James Madison] *except your humble servant my dear Fanny who tho' entirely well your Papa would not suffer me to leave the house. You may guess it goes hard with me to lose a second day of Mrs. Ambler's company who is the same dear affectionate friend she has long been. Nor is her Husband at all changed he rails against eating as usual & kindly takes his five meals a day. I am sure that you will rejoice to hear your firkin arrived the very night before Mrs. Ambler got down so did the buckwheat & we breakfasted comfortably. The sweetmeats have also arrived and I thank you for all most heartily. Poll & her Husband are quite well & send you a deal of love. She is as blithe & more so than I have ever seen her but not a symptom of increasement, Thank Heaven. Mr. Cabell is only troubled about getting a plantation in the upper country which as yet he is not able to do . . . The last Post brought information of the death of Mrs. Jane Walker . . . My thoughts dwell much on the uncertainty of Life & the certainty of Death, but how little avails reflection when Life is spent as tho' Death would never close the Scene.*

Despite her gloom at being made to stay there, Lelia's note conveys the renowned hospitality of the Tucker home, which was more often than not filled with guests. She also gives an example of the moral reflections that were quite common in her letters to her daughters, and reveals a preternatural ability to decipher signs of pregnancy ("increasement") in Polly just two weeks after her wedding.

Letter 53: From Joseph Cabell in Williamsburg to Isaac Coles in Washington

Williamsburg, 26ᵗʰ Jan 1807

Dear Coles:

Your kind letter of 24 ult. [No. 46] has remained so long unanswered on account of my late marriage, of which you may have had notice from the Enquirer, in which some one has thought proper to advertize the public of the great event. Col: Goodwin deserves your thanks and mine, for his attention to the packet, which he left at my brother's in Richmond, at an hour when I was out: he proceeded on his journey before I could find him, in order to make him my acknowledgments. The presents have at length reached their destined owners. I took the liberty of presenting the white one as a new year's gift to my wife. It was a source of affliction to both her & myself that you could not be at our wedding, which was very splendid, and attended by many persons, and among them Henry Tucker from Winchester, Beverley [Tucker] from Charlotte, Wills Cowper from North Carolina, Doctor John Smith from [torn: Gloucester], Bob Gamble from Richmond, and others. None of my Amherst or Richmond relations came down: either from distance, the rigors of the season, or public duties. Well Coles, I am at last a married man, an event which shook my soul so powerfully on anticipation is now a part of the boundless ocean of the past. Are you looking the same way? What are your present plans, and prospects? You cannot complain that I would now assassinate you on the road to Philadelphia. Why are you so silent to me of late, under the flimsy veil of public duties? Do you suppose that my heart has grown cold towards you, because it has been warmed by one, for whom it felt no emotions when we last separated? Can you imagine that amid the rapid incipitudes of my feelings, I am disposed to forget or abandon my oldest and best friends! It is true that in casting my eye over the last six months, I laugh at the wild flights into which my enthusiastic disposition has hurried me. But I see nothing to condemn as criminal, or that ought to produce even a momentary alienation of those friends whom I admitted to the most secret feelings & wishes of my bosom. I am married into a most agreeable family, and to one of the most amiable and affectionate girls on earth. You were under unfavorable impressions towards them when we parted, but I assure you as a man of honor, that they were founded on a mistake. I know not how you obtained your information, but a certain person assures me that she never assigned as a reason for your rejection, that you had maltreated her friend; and the family instead of having changed their opinion of you, still entertain for you their old sentiments of friendship and respect. I require no reply to these remarks; and make them in order that you may hereafter stand on a footing of the most perfect ease with respect to me and mine.

I shall remain here for some time, but shall ultimately settle in the upper country. Write me sometimes, & tell me something about Mr. Barlow, & Fulton. Your Brother Edward is doing well. Your friend.

Joseph C. Cabell

Isaac A. Coles esq.
Secretary to the President [Jefferson]
Washington

A true friend, Cabell dwelt more on Isaac's disappointment in courtship than on his own present and great happiness in that domain. The woman whom Cabell thought had rejected Coles was not named, and that deliberate omission appears to have been a somewhat common practice (recall the earlier letters from Henry St. George to his father, in which Polly was not named). In many letters a blank space or an initial only was placed where the name would normally have appeared in sentences containing sensitive references to that person. Whether naming the subject in such instances was considered bad form, or a risky matter with letters passing through many hands in a household, or was a peculiar precaution taken by just some writers is not clear. Coles did not hesitate to name the mystery woman in his reply.

Letter 54: From Isaac Coles in Washington to Joseph Cabell in Williamsburg

[Washington, undated February 1807] [Note: the opening of this letter is not preserved] . . . *Mr. Randolph is about to retire from public life and he has written to his district to inform his constituents of his determination, so that if you have a mind you may represent us in the next Congress. I cannot say however, "God grant it" as I imagine you feel no desire to commence political life so soon, & as I have reason to believe that Col. Nicholas may be induced to offer himself as a candidate.*

And are you really so delighted with matrimony that you would be disposed to marry your friend whether he is willing or not — and to a Lady too that he has never seen. How gravely you talk of this matter — not only of the Lady, but of her august Mother — but it will not do in spite of your good offices, "nothing can come of it." I would rather serve a whole campaign in Mexico than face that said august personage of whom you speak. The interesting account which I had heard of Miss Helen had excited some desire to know her but nothing more, & the allusion was made to her to convince you of the perfect freedom which I enjoyed & with no other view.

I fear I shall be delayed 10 or 12 days yet by Mr. R. indisposition. I shall not remain here a single day however after the President. It will be May before I return.

Mr. Allen arrived here during the last days of Congress & handed me a letter of introduction from you. I knew him when I lived in Wm'burg & recognized him at once. I was sorry that his stay here should have been at a time when I had not a moment of leisure, & when of course it was out of my power to pay him those little attentions which a stranger is always pleased to receive. – The object of his visit to this place was done away by the rejection of the Bill from the Senate by the lower House, which provides for the raising of an additional body of troops. – I believe he thought it unnecessary to make any application to the war department.

I shall expect to hear from you while I am in Philadelphia about your carriage & will take pleasure in executing any little commission which Mrs. Cabell or Mrs. Tucker may think of in Philadelphia or New York.

Yr friend
I.A. Coles

P.S. I have just seen Gen'l Mason who tells me that we made a mistake about those little Ridicules (or whatever you call them) at last – He has received a letter from Mr. S. directing

him to give them to certain ladies in this place — But this
is a secret between ourselves, as it is all very well as it is - &
if this subsequent order was known, the little purses would
lose all their value with their present owners.

Helen was Helen Skipwith, stepsister of Lelia. Lelia was the
daughter of Sir Peyton Skipwith by his first marriage, to Anne
Miller, who died in 1779; whereas Helen was born to Anne's
sister Jean, who became Sir Peyton's second wife in 1788. The
two were wed in North Carolina to get around a Virginia statute
prohibiting a man from marrying the sister of his deceased wife.
Those unusual elements have combined with others to make
the Skipwith (*neé* Miller) sisters the subject of one of Colonial
Williamsburg's enduring ghost stories.

Here we learn that while Jean's daughter Helen had caught
the eye of Isaac Coles, she had not won or broken his heart, as
Cabell had supposed. Though Isaac did not marry Helen, his
younger brother Tucker Coles did (in 1810). And, to add to
the historical confusion, another younger brother John Coles
later married Helen's younger sister Selina. Cabell could thus
lay a weak claim to success as a Coles-Skipwith matchmaker.
But the only thing he got entirely right was that Jean Miller
was a formidable person. She is remembered to this day for her
library, the largest assembled by a colonial Virginia woman.

As to the last comments regarding *ridicules*, that is indeed
what the small purses, *reticules*, were called by some. Less certain is whether this was a matter of ignorance or poking fun
at the new fashion for women to wear outside their dresses an
article previously worn within. The intrigue between Coles and

Cabell with regard to the ladies destined to receive the ridicules remains a mystery. Coles soon wrote to Cabell again, in reply to his letter of 26th Jan 1807 [No. 53]:

Letter 55: From Isaac Coles in Washington to Joseph Cabell in Williamsburg

Washington, 4th Feb 1807

Dear Cabell,

Altho' I have been much occupied since the commencement of the session by the duties which belong to the situation I now fill, I do not offer this as an Apology for having neglected to write you for some weeks past. It is not "beneath the veil of public duties" that I mean to shelter myself from a reproach I certainly do not deserve. I have not written to you because under the circumstances in which you were placed I thought the obtrusive voice of friendship should not be heard. At such a moment I could have no claims upon your attention. I am not jealous of the fair Being who has lately warmed your heart, but I was unwilling to direct your thoughts even for an instant from her to whom you exclusively belonged. — Besides I had very little to say which would interest you as a man & nothing that my <u>friend</u> w'd be pleased to read. I take little pleasure or interest in the busy scenes which are passing around me, nor have I any plans for the future from which I promise myself much enjoyment. I am going to Philadelphia, New York, &c. it is true, but with no views that can expose me to any *danger on the road. I go merely to satisfy a curiosity which I believe can never be gratified under more favourable circumstances. I have many acquaintances on the way, & promises of all those little civilities w'ch contribute so much to the pleasure of such a tour. An acquaintance which I have lately made with Miss Keene will serve as a passport to every thing interesting in Philadelphia, & altho' it is probable I shall not meet with another Miss K__ in the course of my tour, I shall not be at a loss for agreeable acquaintances. The young lady mentioned to me yesterday that she had received by Post a letter from Mrs. Thompson while in Richmond introducing to her acquaintance a Mr. Cabell who had never, as yet, presented himself & she enquired of me whether I knew any such person. This friend of Mrs. T__ [Tucker] is everything she described her to be. I have never seen a more elegant accomplished woman. She is however a woman of the Great World & rather possessed of those qualities which are calculated to shine in the brilliant circles of fashion than of those which would fit her to pass thro' the varied scenes of life, & to discharge all the duties which may hereafter belong to her as a wife or a mother.*

Of Mssrs. Barlow & Fulton I can tell you very little. They were both of them here a week or ten days ago, but have since returned to Philadelphia, I believe. Mrs. Barlow was in better health than usual & Mr. B__ was himself perfectly well. I met with him frequently in society & he enquired after you with much interest & professed great interest & expressed great pleasure at the prospects that were

opening upon you. Fulton too asked after you. He told me
he had met with you in Europe _ he was civil _ very civil
to me _ but I like him not. He has merit no doubt, but he
seems to me to be a vain, hollow man _ but I forget that
you <u>think</u> him your friend.

Louis Barney sailed a few days ago for the
Mediterranean in a ship belonging to himself & his
Brothers. He thinks it probable he will no return in
two or three years. If you have any commissions for the
Medi'tn he will take great pleasure in executing them
for you. I lately received a letter from our old friend
Wm Lewis who is now a Lieut. In the U.S. Navy on the
Mediterranean Station. He speaks of his old friend Jos.
Cabell in terms of great regard, & begs me to assure you
of the warm attachment he still feels for you.

From Mr. Morton I got a few weeks ago a very long
letter. He mentions that a ship which would sail in some
weeks direct for Virginia wo[uld] *afford* [torn] *opportu-*
nity of writing you & his other friends in your quarter,
[torn] *should avail himself should you wish to write to*
him. Mssrs. Willing & [torn] *Philadelphia will imme-*
diately forward any letters for him which you [torn] *to*
his care. Have you lately heard from Mr. McClure [in
London]*? You were good enough last summer to write*
for a watch for me & I should like very much to know
whether there is any certainty of getting it. I have since
regretted much that the limit had not been 25 or 30 guin-
eas, instead of 12. Was your letter imperative, or was it

a little commission which Mr. McC might execute if he should accidentally meet with a good opportunity of conveying the watch to you. Write me, for if you think it will not be sent I will furnish myself in Philadelphia or New York.

I am much pleased to hear that you think of fixing yourself in the upper country & I hope it will be on that part of it in which I shall probably reside. Believe me Cabell, the idea that the intercourse which has always subsisted between us will ever continue, is one of those to which I look forward with most pleasure and is one which I can never give up. I have ever felt for you the attachment of a brother, I never have, I hope I never shall have occasion to think of you otherwise.

I have only paper enough left to request you to present me very respectfully to yr wife & to Mrs. Tucker.

Yr friend

I. A. Coles

In addition to conveying the depth of the friendship between Coles and Cabell, the above letter perfectly reveals the expectation that friends travelling to other places would offer to carry out "commissions," be they social or commercial, for their relatives and friends. Coles did not hesitate to find and purchase a horse-drawn carriage for Cabell, or to seek out any item his new wife and mother-in-law might wish from the commercial centers of Philadelphia and New York. Conversely, Cabell had fulfilled the expectation that he write letters of introduction for Coles to any acquaintance residing in the places that his friend planned to visit, so that they might provide him with hospitality.

Both of those social practices again found a place in Cabell's following reply to Isaac, but they were not foremost in his thoughts.

Letter 56: From Joseph C. Cabell in Williamsburg to Isaac A. Coles in Washington

Williamsburg, 17th Feb 1807

Dear Coles,

In consequence of your telling me in yours of the 4th inst., for which I return you my sincere thanks, that you are going to the northward, I am left to conclude that you mean to set off before long, and I therefore enclose three letters of introduction, which will be of service to you, were you going even without secret views, that you profess not to entertain. After all, I cannot help suspecting that mere idle curiosity is not a proper motive to move a man like you. Perhaps you are trying to conceal your views not only from the knowledge of your friends, but are endeavoring to assume the calm feelings with which you would act, were you not conscious of them. I will lay a wager with you that you cast many an oblique glance at Miss K. [Keene] or some other Northern Belle. Whatever may be your inducements, my dear Coles, my heart travels with you, interests itself in your wishes, will weep at your disappointments, and rejoice in your success. I need not tell you that you ought not to be captivated by the glittering accomplishments of the <u>sea port</u> girls, to whom the movements, and pleasures of large cities have become physical wants, unless you may be disposed to leave us, for life, which I should infinitely deplore. I need not tell you, that a brilliant, fashionable wife, is a very pretty thing, like a rainbow; of no use very often but to delight the eye, and its beauties vanishing with the first change of scenery. But you require no counsel from me. Perhaps it is even impertinent in me to say a word on the subject. Especially as I sat down with the intention of requesting you to destroy all the letters I have written you since I came home on the subject of women. As I am now a sober married man, I have no wish to preserve these traces of the tempestuous feelings of my single state. I should be sorry for them to fall into other hands than your own; or for a knowledge of their contents to spread beyond the few whom I made my confidential friends. Do not suppose from this, that I am retiring a step from you: no, this will never be. But others know me not, as well as you do. When you go to Philadelphia, it might be curious to observe, were you to fall in with any of those I know there, whether my motives for returning were suspected. Beyond this, I am not inquisitive to know anything about them. – In a kind letter I lately received from Irving, he congratulates me on my happy marriage: tells me, he was apprehensive of the issue of my proposed journey; and jeers me as to my <u>philosophic</u>, <u>platonic</u> affections.

For some time past I have observed with much regret a melancholy strain running thro' your letters, whenever you speak of yourself and your views in life. I see nothing to justify such gloomy ideas, and hope you will keep a watchful eye on the tendency of your feelings. You must not continue longer than this year at Washington, but retire after your return from the north, the some definite course of life. You must settle in the Upper country, not far from me, and join me in the laborious habits to which I mean to dedicated the remnant of my life. I should be cruelly mortified to be disappointed in this scheme, so near to my heart, and so intimately connected with my future happiness.

I wrote positively for your watch, and should my letter reach Maclure, I have no doubt of his sending it. But you might easily dispose of it should you not like it. Indeed mine is not as good as I thought, and I would advise you to send for another. I shall write to Maclure before long, & countermand the order. I have not received a line from him since I returned to this country. I shall be much pleased to receive the promised letter from Morton, and may avail myself of the politeness of his correspondents in Philadelphia. Had I known of Barney's sailing, I would have troubled him with some letter, and commission to Mr. Walsh for some wine. How do you make your remittances to him? Should you write again to our good friend Lewis, I hope you present him on my part with assurances of my gratitude for his recollection of me while on distant seas. Tell him I never erase a name from the list of my old friends.

I leave this tomorrow on a short visit of about a week to my Brother in Richmond, and while there shall take measures for procuring some sort of vehicle for conveying my wife to see my friends in the upper country during the summer. Should you go immediately on to Philadelphia, perhaps, you would do me the favor to purchase one for me; in which I would give you the description, and send you the money necessary in due time. For this, & other reasons, I will be thankful, if you will immediately drop me a line at Richmond, informing me as to the time of your setting out.

We are about making an attempt towards the foundation of a museum naturae, under the auspices of a society for the promotion of the natural sciences in Virginia, which will commence at this place, and consist chiefly of the Professors of the College, but may hereafter be removed to a more central situation, and embrace a wider sphere. I enclose you a paper written and published by Mr. Girardin, and ingenious Frenchman, & the successor of Mr. Bellini, with the view of directing the public mind to this interesting subject. As soon as the plan shall have been drawn up, I will send it to you; and shall expect you to become a member, and lend your aid towards it. Could you not procure us the powerful assistance of Mr. Jefferson's good will & influence. The thing is in its infancy, and you shall hear more of it in future. In the interim, I am not very sanguine, but shall do all I can towards bringing it into life. It is time Virginians should dispel the shades that hover over our country. Mrs. T. & her daughter return very sincerely their thanks for your kind message to them. Your friend. Joseph C. Cabell.

Isaac A. Coles, Esq,
Secretary to the President

The full measure of the longstanding friendship between Cabell and Coles is revealed in this letter. Sincerity, concern, teasing, and warmth are all in play at once. The sentiment, *". . . my heart travels with you, interests itself in your wishes, will weep at your disappointments, and rejoice in your success,"* was expressed by Joseph but true of both men.

The Irving who is mentioned is Washington Irving, later to be known as "the father of American literature." Cabell first met him while both men were in Europe just a few years earlier. They became instant friends, traveled through Italy, Switzerland and France together, and met again in Irving's home city of New York upon Cabell's return. It appears that Irving, like Coles and many others, had just months earlier been assured by Cabell of his "philosophic and platonic" views on women or marriage. We are never told just what ideas "on the subject of women" he now regretted having expressed. But all who heard or read his prior pronouncements were now greatly entertained by the fact he was married and wanted the "tempestuous traces" of those recent declarations to be destroyed or forgotten. Cabell's dizzying change of mind and course was the source of affectionate laughs and jeers from family and friends, from well beyond Richmond to Washington and New York.

Conclusion

The curtain was raised for this account with a long letter from Cabell, revealing his thoughts as an anxious suitor. Now, only a few months later, he was by his own description "a sober married man." In the days and weeks following the wedding he continued to address the large questions of how to earn a living and where to settle with Polly, and such practical concerns as how to travel now that he could not simply jump on a horse and ride off by himself. With the drama of his betrothal and marriage behind him, his mind and efforts were decidedly directed toward his future with his wife, his family, and his friends.

The curtain now falls with words from a letter written by one of those many friends. In 1833, more than twenty-five years after these events, and only weeks before his own death, William Wirt wrote a letter to William Cabell recalling their great mutual friend, Dr. William Hare. The amiable doctor died in 1818 but still loomed as large in Wirt's memory as he had years before at Christmastime of 1806 in the living room of the Governor's Richmond home. It was there, in those wintry days, when all in the family were cheerfully raising their glasses to celebrate "Jo and his Polly." Wirt's words give life to the scenes then, and to the whole story. They show his gift as a writer and give us a gift as readers. It is fitting that we end this treasury of historic letters with them.

Last Letter: From William Wirt in Baltimore
to William H. Cabell in Richmond[m]

Christmas Day, 1833

*"A merry Christmas to you, my dear Cabell, and to all
your fireside! I said to Mrs. Wirt just now, 'Let us send for
Dr. Hare and Cabell to help us make egg-nog for our company.' Poor dear Hare! Do you remember how delighted
he was with his occupation at our sideboard, in the dining
room of our white house in Richmond? How he would talk
and beat away, and laugh, and walk across the room occasionally to the fireplace! I think I can see him now, every
moment hear his voice, see his dry funny smile, and smack
of his lips on tasting the egg-nog – and the wise shake of
his head – 'It is mighty near right, but not quite: I think
it wants a little more spirit – what do you think, Mr.
Cabell?' Bless his old heart, I say again! Alas! How long
has it been since that excellent heart has ceased to beat! Oh
world! world! this poor bargain of life! If bargain it may
be called in which we had no voice. Yet what an excellent
bargain we used to think it in those days when we were in
the prime of our manhood, doing well, and all our friends
living and smiling around us!"*

—ᘉ—

Epilogue

Many persons in this real-life drama went on to lead illustrious lives as public figures. This epilogue does not touch on those public careers. It simply sheds a little light on what later happened in the private lives of the main characters *after* the winter of 1806-1807.

Joseph and Polly (Mary Walker) Cabell settled in Nelson County in the upper country and remained married for almost fifty years. Joseph died in 1856 and Mary in 1862. They lived the entire time at Edgewood, a plantation that Joseph purchased and expanded. They had no children, apparently as a result of a miscarriage suffered by Mary early in their marriage. But in 1825, they became the guardians and parents of Rebecca Parke Farley Carter, the nine-year-old orphaned daughter of Mary's brother, Dr. Charles Carter. Rebecca became the light of their lives but died of illness in 1839, at the age of twenty-three.

Dr. Charles Carter completed his medical education but chose not to practice. Rather he settled on the half of the Corotoman estate that became his in 1813 when it was divided between him and Joseph Cabell, as the husband of Mary. Charles married Elizabeth (Betsy) Corbin in 1814 and they had three children. Waves of tragedy washed over him beginning in 1824, when Betsy and their two sons died. Charles died soon after, leaving Rebecca as an orphan. Joseph Cabell happened to be visiting Corotoman in the fall of 1825, when he discovered and then stayed with Charles in the final days of his illness.

St. George Tucker and Lelia Tucker spent most, if not all, of their summers with Joseph and Polly at Edgewood, after the young couple moved there in 1808. In 1823 they left Williamsburg permanently and moved to Edgewood, where they dwelt for the rest of their lives in a separate cottage built for them near the main house. The main house was destroyed by a fire in 1955, but the Tucker cottage still stands. St. George died at Edgewood in 1827; Lelia in 1834. Their graves lie next to those of Joseph and Mary Cabell, and Rebecca Parke Farley Carter in the family graveyard at Edgewood.

William and Agnes Cabell moved from Richmond to Nelson County in 1810 to an estate which William purchased and then named Montevideo. Financial troubles led him to sell it and return to Richmond in 1821, where the family remained for the rest of their lives. During the entire time William continued to serve on the Court of Appeals, sitting with both St. George Tucker and John Coalter during part of his long tenure. In 1851 he retired from the Court after forty years, and died two years later. Agnes died in 1863, having brought eight children into the world with William during their forty-five years of marriage.

John and Fannie (Ann Francis Randolph Tucker) Coalter lived at their plantation Elm Grove in Staunton, with Fannie struggling to manage it most of the time because of her husband's prolonged absences as a judge. In 1809 St. George Tucker Coalter was born, joining his sisters Elizabeth and

Frances Lelia, mentioned in this account. Four years later, Fannie died at the age of thirty-four. In 1822 John Coalter married Hannah Williamson and moved to Chatham, their estate near Fredericksburg. He died there in 1838.

Henry St. George and Evelina Tucker lived in Winchester for all of their lives. In great contrast to his discouraging and lonely opening years in what was then a remote town, Henry went on to a life of many accomplishments in what became a city. He opened and taught at his own law school in Winchester, was on the law faculty at William & Mary, was later appointed as the Professor of Law at the University of Virginia, and was elected to the U.S. Congress. Henry and Evelina had twelve children. Henry died in 1848 and Evelina in 1855.

—w—

On Palace Green - The Cast of Characters

The principal characters are here introduced as they were *at the time of the story*. I say no more about them than they could have said themselves in the winter of 1806-1807, when the events in these letters occurred. While *we* now know much of what happened during the rest of their lives, *they* certainly did not know what would happen even the next day.

Joseph Carrington Cabell (b. 1778) – Cabell (pronounced "cabble") was a student at William Mary from 1796 to 1798, and again two years later when he returned to attend the renowned lectures in law being given by St. George Tucker. Like Charles, Cabell was often ill in his youth and was advised to travel to Europe to improve his health. He departed in early 1803 and traveled widely in France, Italy, Switzerland and England. He kept a daily journal in which he made extensive notes on the geology, agriculture, manufacturing, and other aspects of the places he visited. He returned in the summer of 1806 and was boarding at the home of his brother William in Richmond when, just a few months later, this story opened.

William H. Cabell (b. 1772) – William was Joseph's older brother. He too graduated from William & Mary but, unlike Joseph, did so with a law degree. At the time of this account he had been elected to his second of three one-year terms as the Governor of Virginia, and was living in Richmond with his wife Agnes and their two children. There were two other Cabell brothers, Nicholas and George, but William and Joseph were the closest, corresponding and helping each other regularly on many matters. At this time, Joseph constantly turned for advice to William, who took great enjoyment in delivering it emphatically to his little brother.

St. George Tucker (b. 1752) – Having emigrated to Virginia from Bermuda, St. George was a member of the General Court and Professor of Law at William & Mary when he married Lelia. By the winter of 1807 he had left the college to sit on the Court of Appeals, the state's highest court, which met in Richmond. His annotated edition of William Blackstone's *Commentaries on the Laws of England* (1803) had become the definitive text on American law. Conversely, his *Dissertation on Slavery* (1796), which argued that Virginia should put an end to the immoral institution and proposed a way to do it, was ignored by the Assembly. Hundreds of loving letters between St. George and his children, as well as many published and unpublished poems, reveal his greatest joy to be that of being their father.

Lelia Skipwith (Carter) Tucker (b. 1767) – A daughter of Sir Peyton Skipwith, Lelia grew up on the family estate of *Prestwould* in Mecklenburg County. In 1784 she married George Carter (age 22), a young Revolutionary War veteran, and moved to his *Corotoman* estate in Lancaster County. He died just four years later, leaving Lelia with their two infants, Charles and Mary. In

1791 she married St. George Tucker and moved to his home in Williamsburg, where she embraced and thrived on the social life. The great hospitality of St. George and Lelia was remarked upon by many, with their Williamsburg home ever open to guests and filled with them more often than not.

Mary Walker Carter (b. 1788) – Mary, called 'Polly' by all, grew up in the Tucker house from the age of three, when she moved there with her mother and brother Charles. When this story opens she was eighteen, and one of the belles of Williamsburg who caught the attention of various young men. She traveled occasionally to visit family and friends, in particular her grandfather Charles Carter and his family at Shirley plantation near Richmond. Though no letter penned by Polly during this chapter in her life survives, the image of her as a confident, attractive, and beloved member of the Tucker household is clear from other sources. Her bond with her stepfather was deep and mutual.

Charles Carter (b. 1786) – When Charles was taken to Williamsburg in 1791 at the age of five he joined the five children of St. George and his first wife who were already there. He was closest in both age and temperament to his new stepbrother Beverley (Nathaniel Beverley), who later described himself as rebellious as a youth. Charles was often ill and was not a diligent student. In 1805 he was warned of possible dismissal from William & Mary due to his absences. Soon thereafter he was put on a ship bound for England, in order for him to pursue at the University of Edinburgh his avowed interest in becoming a doctor. Leaving the American climate was also seen as way to relieve his illnesses. He was in Paris at the time of this story.

John Coalter (b. 1769) At the time of this story John Coalter had been married to Polly's older stepsister, Ann Frances Bland Tucker (Fannie), since 1802. He first met Fannie in 1788 when she was nine years old, and he had moved from his family's home in Augusta County to live with the Tuckers as a tutor. In exchange for this service, St. George arranged for Coalter to study law at William & Mary, from which he obtained his law degree in 1790 and returned to Augusta to practice. Fannie was his third wife, the two preceding having died in childbirth. The Coalters gave St. George and Lelia their first grandchildren, Frances Lelia and Elizabeth.

John Hartwell Cocke (b. 1780) – Cocke attended William and Mary at the same time as Cabell. They there formed a close friendship based especially upon their shared love of the natural sciences and agriculture. Cocke grew up on the Mount Pleasant estate, sixteen miles as the crow flies from Williamsburg, but on the south side of the James River. In 1802 he married Anne Blaws Barraud, daughter of Dr. Philip Barraud, a close Williamsburg friend and neighbor of the Tuckers. At the time of this story, the couple were in the lengthy process of leaving the tidewater area for *Bremo,* an estate that Cocke was developing on the upper James. It would put them in the upper country where the Cabells had long been established.

Henry St. George Tucker (b. 1780) – Henry was the oldest of the three sons born to St. George and his first wife, Frances Bland Randolph. Both parents were assiduous about their children's education and studious Henry more than met their expectations. After obtaining his law degree from William & Mary he moved to Winchester in 1803, at the behest of his father, to try to establish a practice. Charles was sent to spend the summer with him in 1804 in the hope that the older stepbrother might inspire the younger by example. It led instead to great frustration for them both. By the time of this story Henry was finding success in both his work and personal life in Winchester, after his difficult first years of disappointment in both.

Col. Henry Skipwith (b. 1751) – Henry was Lelia's uncle, the brother of her father. A veteran of the Revolution, he was also a brother-in-law of Thomas Jefferson, both men having married daughters of John Wayles. Skipwith first lived with Ann (*nee* Wayles) in Cumberland County, where they built their home *Hors du Monde*. Following Ann's death in 1798, he married Elizabeth Byrd and moved with her to Williamsburg around 1801. They lived in Wythe House, a brick mansion across the Palace Green from the Tucker house, which Skipwith purchased from George Wythe, first Professor of Law at William & Mary. 'Uncle Henry' was full of fun and energy, and was especially liked by Charles.

William Wirt (b. 1772) – Born and schooled in Maryland, in 1795 Wirt began his career in law in Virginia. After the death of his first wife in 1799 he moved from their home near Charlottesville to Richmond. There he met and married in 1802 Elizabeth Gamble, the sister of William Cabell's wife Agnes, and they moved to Norfolk. By the time of this story they had returned to Richmond, where Wirt set up a private law practice and earned a reputation as both an eloquent courtroom orator and author. His well-received, fictional "Letters of the British Spy" were first published in the Virginia Argus, a weekly newspaper, and then in book form in 1805. His relationship with the Cabells was that of an intimate friend and relative.

Isaac A. Coles (b. 1780) Like Cabell, Coles had been a student at William and Mary, and was from an old established family of Albemarle County. Indeed, his middle initial is said to stand for 'Albemarle', having been created by Coles to distinguish himself from two other relatives with the same name. Coles and Cabell corresponded often and at times on matters of the heart, with Coles regarding Cabell as a brother. They were together in London for a while during Cabell's European tour. Isaac became a member of the bar and practiced law in his home county before being asked by his neighbor, President Thomas Jefferson, to serve as his personal secretary. That is the position he held at the time of this story.

Illustrations

Image 1. *Portrait of Joseph Carrington Cabell.* Courtesy of Special Collections, University of Virginia Library, Charlottesville, Va. http://search.lib.virginia.edu.catalogue/uva-lib:2159813.

Image 2. *Portrait of Judge William H. Cabell.* Courtesy of Special Collections, University of Virginia Library, Charlottesville, Va. http://search.lib.virginia.edu.catalogue/uva-lib:2159819.

Image 3. *Miniature Portrait of St. George Tucker,* Pierre Henri, Virginia, probably 1799, watercolor on ivory, accession #2007-45, 1, image #D2007-CMD-0283. Courtesy of *The Colonial Williamsburg Foundation, Museum Purchase, The Friends of Colonial Williamsburg Collections Fund.*

Image 4. *Portrait of Lelia Skipwith Carter Tucker,* Pierre Henri, Virginia, probably 1799, watercolor on ivory, accession #2007-45, 2, image #D2007-CMD-0284. Courtesy of *The Colonial Williamsburg Foundation, Museum Purchase, The Friends of Colonial Williamsburg Collections Fund.*

Image 5. *The Swan Tavern, Richmond.* Courtesy of The Virginia Historical Society.

Image 6. *Plot of the City of Williamsburg, Virginia* drawn by Benjamin Bucktrout, August 1800, and sketched by Robert A. Lively, December 1867. Courtesy of *Special Collections, John D. Rockefeller Jr. Library, The Colonial Williamsburg Foundation.*

Endnotes

a. Letter 1. *The Papers of Joseph C. Cabell and the Cabell Family*, Albert and Shirley Small Special Collections Library, University of Virginia. Accession Number 38-111, Box 4.

   Note: Unless otherwise cited the original copies of the letters transcribed in this book are held in the above collection and box.

   All of the letters but the last were transcribed by the author from the originals. I have preserved the spelling, punctuation and other elements of the letters as written, with the exception that the date lines and closings have been put into a common form. Within the letters, any notes added by me are placed in square brackets.

b. Letter 7. *Tucker Coleman Papers, 1664-1945*, Special Collections, Earl Gregg Swem Library, William & Mary College, Mss. 40 T79, Box 25.

c. Letter 8. *Tucker Coleman Papers, 1664-1945*, Special Collections, Earl Gregg Swem Library, William & Mary College, Mss. 40 T79, Box 25.

d. The information on both The Eagle and The Swan taverns is largely derived from:

Gish, Agnes Evans. *Virginia Taverns, Ordinaries and Coffee Houses: 18th–Early 19th Century Entertainment Along the Buckingham Road*, Willow Bend Books, 2005, p.168-205.

e. Mutual Assurance Society of Virginia declaration issued to Dr. James Currie on 15 February 1796 for the Eagle Tavern, Richmond. Online Catalog, Library of Virginia, http://image.lva.virginia.gov/cgi-bin/GetMU.pl?dir=0525/C0023&card=107 Document Image

f. The Virginia Historical Register, and Literary Advertiser, Volume 2, 1849, p. 160

g. Letter 34. *Tucker Coleman Papers, 1664-1945*, Special Collections, Earl Gregg Swem Library, William & Mary College, Mss. 40 T79, Box 26.

h. Letter 42. Manuscripts and Archives Division, The New York Public Library. "Letter to [Fulwar Skipwith, Consul General of the United States, Paris.]" *The New York Public Library Digital Collections.* 1798. http://digitalcollections.nypl.org/items/be97b4b1-6a1d-725d-e040-e00a1806751a

i. Letter 44. *Papers of the Joseph Carrington Cabell Family*, Albert and Shirley Small Special Collections Library, University of Virginia, Accession Number 38-111c, Box 4. **Note:** Accession number 38-111c is separate from 38-111, which contains most of the letters.

j. Letter 47. *Tucker Coleman Papers, 1664-1945*, Special Collections, Earl Gregg Swem Library, William & Mary College, Mss. 40 T79, Box 26.

k. Letter 48. *Tucker Coleman Papers, 1664-1945*, Earl Gregg Swem Library, William & Mary College. Mss. 40 T79, Box 26.

l. Letter 52. *Tucker Coleman Papers, 1664-1945*, Special Collections, Earl Gregg Swem Library, William & Mary College, Mss. 40 T79, Box 26.

m. Last Letter. Brown, Alexander. *The Cabells And Their Kin. A Memorial Volume of History, Biography, And Genealogy*, Houghton, Mifflin & Co., Boston and New York,1895, p.262. Reprinted by HardPress Publishing, 8345 NW 66th Street, #2561, Miami, Florida 33166, 2013. ISBN: 9781313070140.

Made in the USA
Columbia, SC
09 July 2018